LIFE ON ROUTE 66

LIFE ON ROUTE 66

PERSONAL ACCOUNTS ALONG THE MOTHER ROAD TO CALIFORNIA

CLAUDIA & ALAN HELLER

THE History PRESS

Published by The History Press
Charleston, SC 29403
www.historypress.net

Cover images: girl with dog in black-and-white courtesy of Sue Ellen Willis; photo with three boys in hotrod courtesy of Fred Johnson; center photo of road courtesy of Ronan Murray, ©2011; all other images by Alan Heller.

Images by Alan Heller unless otherwise indicated.

First published 2012

Manufactured in the United States

ISBN 978.1.60949.622.7

Library of Congress CIP data applied for.

For our children:

Holiday Jean
Beau Garrett
Jenner Alan

Contents

Foreword

Being involved in the Route 66 community, we all monitor the media, checking on articles that highlight the people, places and events. A few years ago, there was a very nice article with good photos—Claudia wrote and Alan took the photos, yes a wife/husband team. It was obvious that they had done their homework and caught the true meaning of the road. Over the next few years, I not only got to read more of their journeys on the road but also came to respect their work.

Watching them grow into real "roadies" and get more involved in the road was a real treat for me. There is a magical magnet that draws people and holds them that is hard to explain but easy to understand once you accept that you, too, are caught in the grip of the road. As they progressed on their search of just what this old road is all about, by visiting the places and meeting the people that make up the culture of this national/international icon, they became not only fans but also promoters of the road.

So here is another book on the road with photos of Route 66. But wait, I did not know that fact or that person, and is that photo of someplace on the road I haven't seen? Each one of us who travels the road sees it in a different way, and sometimes we capture it in our words and photos that could only happen right at that time and place. Then, being able to share those moments where we created a lasting memory is a talent that not everyone has. Claudia and Alan have it. And you will see it with every word you read and photo you look at in this book.

The road is a better place because we gain folks like this into our family. I am pleased to know them and honored to call them my friends and fellow roadies.

Jim Conkle
Publisher, Editor
Route 66 Pulse
Mother Road Enterprises

Acknowledgements

A multitude of thanks go out to those who encouraged and assisted us in this project.

Pia Orense, my editor at the *Highlander* newspaper, for assigning us to a project that enriched our lives.

Alex and Mirna de Lira Lopez, of DLL Business Solutions in Duarte, California, for their technical help.

Jim Conkle, editor of the *Route 66 Pulse* newspaper, for his encouragement and kindness in writing the foreword to this book.

Authors David G. Clark, Jim Hinckley, Joe de Kehoe, Michael Patris, Elizabeth Pomeroy, Dave Emerson, Scott Piotrowski and Diane Wilson for their words of wisdom.

The staffs at the Route 66 museums in Victorville and Barstow, California.

The many readers of the newspapers distributed by the San Gabriel Valley Newspaper Group who selflessly shared their memories of the Mother Road and/or family journals depicting the joys and hardships encountered on the road.

My father, Lewis Garrett, whose research was helpful and who passed down to me the gene that instilled a passion for travel and writing!

My sister, Karen Garrett, who graciously donated her proofreading skills.

And finally, Sheri Uhlig, who handcrafted a quilt out of Route 66 material to keep us cozy on our travels.

Introduction

When my editor asked me to write a series of articles on Route 66 for publication in the *Highlander* newspaper, I immediately said yes. Living near the route in Duarte, I was somewhat familiar with the road's history and throughout the years had poked around many of the Mother Road towns in the Mojave Desert, communities that had blossomed and withered over the years. I had no idea at the time that this project would provide an outlet for readers eager to share personal memories of their experiences on the road.

Following the logical westward migration on the route, the series began with an article about Needles, the route's California-Arizona border town. My husband, Alan, and I had visited the town many times, photographing the historical Route 66 landmarks. We were fortunate to take a tour of the withering El Garces Hotel. Time and again, we returned to the border community to gather current information and photos, following which the article practically wrote itself. Shortly after it was published, the unforeseen occurred. A series of events emerged, sparking renewed enthusiasm for me and the readers.

Readers who were bursting with memories of their experiences along the road during its early days began contacting me. Many, now seniors, recalled backseat adventures as they traveled Route 66 with their parents. Others relayed stories handed down by family members, and one reader had long coveted a detailed journal penned by her great uncle detailing his trip west in 1927. She longed to share its contents with those who would appreciate it.

These heartfelt and often thrilling stories continued arriving and are described in detail in this book. The examples are many. There is the son who recalled that his father hitchhiked west from Kansas only to be turned around at the California border by the authorities "because there were already too many unemployed men in California." And another boy, now a senior living in La Verne, vividly remembered fearing an attack by Indians as he, then six years old, and his sister rode a Greyhound bus across Arizona.

I heard from Manny Avila of Hacienda Heights, who has throughout the years kept in contact with his old buddy, Dick Sproul, often reminiscing about their adventures along the road in 1946. Fresh home from World War II, these "boys" took a merchant marine ship from Los Angeles to New York, and after hearing Nat King Cole sing "Route 66," they bought a "rag top" and drove home on the Mother Road, a trip rife with memorable events. A father-son bond was renewed when Frank Ayala of Huntington Park drove his son, Xavy, along Route 66 en route to Michigan, where Xavy was to start college. As they crossed the California-Arizona border at Needles, the young man asked his father a question that proved to be prophetic in the context of the Mother Road.

Research into the place names of the San Bernardino County towns along the route, many of which have disappeared, revealed why my own father would often leave our Hollywood Hills home and vanish into the desert for days at a time. A contact from Sue Ellen Willis of Covina relayed her happy childhood memories of the family's life in several desert communities as they followed her father, a railway worker, along the tracks. Kenneth Pitzer recalled that as a child the family toted a shovel on their Route 66 treks to dig the car out of holes along the way. Lonell Spencer of Arcadia recalled fond memories of carrying his bride, Marguerite, over the threshold of their honeymoon room teepee at the Wigwam Motel in Rialto.

Socks were the only items Fred Johnson of Covina packed when he and his buddies traveled the road in a 1930 Ford roadster, a trip of a lifetime for a seventeen-year-old boy. The year was 1947.

Details about these and other stories are set forth in the California Route 66 section of this book, basically reprints of the articles published in a fifteen-month newspaper series.

CHICAGO OR BUST

In early 2010, my husband and I made a decision to drive "America's Highway" to Chicago in celebration of our sixty-sixth birthdays and our pending retirements. We started making the arrangements, purchased a used eighteen-foot trailer and notified our employers. We would leave on June 23 and, without a strict schedule, travel the road with the aim of returning by August 20 in time for the second birthday of our youngest granddaughter, Kirra. We made return visits to the Route 66 museums in Victorville and Barstow for maps, guidebooks and advice. And of course, we needed a CD with Route 66 music, banners, pins, T-shirts and other memorabilia. Probably our most useful purchase was Jerry McClanahan's *EZ Guide to Route 66*, which I had to read backward because we were traveling from west to east rather than the traditional east–west trek.

Leaving home for two months requires an abundance of planning. Paying bills may be set up on line, but that leaves a number of anticipated chores: watering the yard, picking up mail and errant papers and maintaining the pool, and what was I going to do with Chewy, my seventeen-year-old blind and deaf dog? Little by little, the chores were assigned to family, friends and neighbors to whom I am deeply indebted, especially to my granddaughter, Sierra, for taking responsibility for Chewy.

After months of planning and anticipation, the day came and we headed east. For a time, I would have to abandon my weekly California Route 66 *Highlander* newspaper series, which by that time had covered Needles to Fontana, and switch to articles on U.S. Route 66. Upon our return, I would continue with the California series starting where I had left off, Rancho Cucamonga, and then continue on to Santa Monica. On June 23, 2010, trailer packed to the hilt, we headed east with Nat King Cole blasting on the CD player.

It was soon evident that writing a single article on each of the seven Route 66 states on our trip would not suffice. There was too much to see and report. Each day for a month, we would rise early, sit outside, sip our coffee and plan the day's events. Using the *EZ Guide* and other maps, pamphlets and books, we marked the route, loosely planning where to stop. Abandoning the interstate and driving on the Old Route had its advantages. Cruising at fifty-five miles per hour was more relaxing and safer with a trailer in tow. While cars flew by at eighty miles per hour on the interstate, we took our time and enjoyed the view, ever aware that the purpose of the trip was the journey, not the destination. Often, when we stopped to take a photo, it wasn't necessary to pull over—we would simply stop and shoot away.

We became acutely aware of the old motels and cafés, some of which were in ruins, others eking out continuing business. Abandoned buildings melted into the ground like Mayan ruins, covered with vines, debris and graffiti. The hopes and dreams of entrepreneurs answering the call for roadside services when Route 66 invaded town were dashed when the interstate lured away fickle drivers. After the route's dedication in 1926, townsfolk along the way capitalized on the growing needs of motorists. Mom, who had cooked for her family, was now cooking for carloads of travelers, famished after a day on the road. Kids were piled into one bedroom, while their rooms were rented to travelers seeking shelter for the night. Dad, who tinkered in his garage, became a mechanic, answering the prayers of motorists in need of repairs, tires and maintenance. Thousands of cars passed through these small towns each day, and eventually businesses began to vie for tourist dollars by conjuring up the most outrageous roadside attractions. The bigger the attraction the better! Overnight they sprung up—the giant cross, leaning tower, muffler man, totem, whale, Cadillac graveyard and the like—calling out to motorists suffering from boredom or simply satisfying their curiosity.

With the demise of the Mother Road, hundreds of the attractions decayed or were carried off, but many remain and are affectionately cared for by city staff, businesses or private owners. In some cases, private owners, recognizing the historic significance of the gem in their care, open their property to the public, foreign and domestic, allowing tourists to visit and photograph the icons of the road.

Along the road, we met many tourists visiting from other countries. The Dutch Route 66 Club sponsors a road trip every year, idolizing the Mother Road as a path to truth and freedom. In Kingman, we met a group of Germans traveling the road, two of whom shared our last name. In Kansas, we talked briefly with a couple from France, traveling the road just as we were. It has become a "cult" highway, beckoning visitors to enjoy its treasures and lore.

In the 1920s, the automobile had improved to a point that people would take road trips for myriad reasons. Fleeing the Dust Bowl and the depressed job market was, of course, one scenario. Others were simply following the promise of a better life in California, a dream that was often elusive. As automobiles became more reliable, the American love for travel reigned, and many people took to the road, some simply to visit the wonders of the nation. The linking of preexisting roads to form a continuous highway was a novel idea, one that made travel more feasible. But the road was not what we think of today as a new highway. Much of it was dirt or gravel, filled with hazards. In the Texas range land, drivers had to stop and open fences that spanned the road and close them after passing. Road maintenance was not very effective, and areas would wash out in heavy rains. There was a time when young men in Kansas were required by law to maintain the road on a volunteer basis.

This book is not merely an account of the rise, fall and resurrection of the Mother Road; it has more lofty goals. I wish to pay tribute to those who have honestly and with conviction shared their personal experiences on the road. I hope to encourage anyone with an interest to travel the Old Route on sections close to home or all the way to Chicago. It is my aim to set an example to retirees and others who may have dreamed about but suppressed a desire to seek adventure on the road. This mystical road beckons to the young and old alike, to those who may want to travel in an RV or car and to those who have months to spend or merely a short vacation.

Part I

Life on California's Route 66

Why Travel the Mother Road?

Its heyday has flourished and waned, and yet Route 66, the 2,400-mile corridor from the Midwest through Los Angeles, continues to fascinate travelers with a promise of adventure, nostalgia and dreams fulfilled. Today it is called America's Highway.

Why does a mere ribbon of asphalt hold appeal not only for those who live in America but also for people worldwide? Why do more and more travelers forsake modern multilane highways to trek leisurely on historic Route 66 between Chicago and California? Now antiquated, the highway, which has been dubbed the Mother Road, is rife with myths and truths, successes and failures. For decades, it sparked innovative enterprises that took root in a more innocent time.

No longer a primary commerce route, it has lost its place as the blood flow of American travel. Today, the road beckons history buffs and boasts icons that reflect stories of its past. Somewhere deep down there must be evidence of tire tracks left by autos that traversed the road against all odds. As optimistic travelers headed west, families and businesses along the way scrambled to fill the blossoming demand for overnight accommodations and meals.

Motels and eateries flourished, and the road took on a life of its own. Born in 1926, the glory of Route 66 thrived until modern freeways demoted it to a second-class road. No longer did travelers amble along its pavement, frequenting eateries and motels at a leisurely pace. Gone were the days when families in towns lining the road opened their doors to motorists in need of a bed and meal.

Modern multilane freeways, with tempting fifty-five-mile-per-hour signs, rendered moot the saying "It is not the destination, but the journey." Suddenly, the latter became all important and the former passé. However, Route 66 has refused to fade away. In this age of computers, cellphones and SUVs, America's Highway has gained a following of folks who celebrate its history and yearn to follow it back to a friendlier and more easygoing day.

My husband and I found great pleasure in reliving the days of the Mother Road, whether sleeping in a wigwam, photographing a juice stand in the shape of an orange or perusing photographs of movie stars on the walls of the eateries they once patronized. We have traveled on the road, over it and under it.

From time to time, the Gold Road Mine in Arizona offers tours, guiding visitors through a century-old mine shaft that winds below Route 66. The mine is located near the burro-friendly Route 66 town of Oatman.

Following the road, I feel the anticipation and trepidation that consumed the Joads, so aptly described in John Steinbeck's historical novel *The Grapes of Wrath*. In those days, one did not traverse the desert during hot daylight hours, and maps were not accurate. Radiators boiled over. Tires went flat. Food was scarce and competition fierce. And yet family after family rumbled over the highway to find a better life in the West.

Today, many of the route's icons have disappeared, but Route 66 still offers adventures and opportunities for travelers to relive its former glory. Day trips from western San Bernardino County to the road's terminus in Santa Monica will take you back to in time and can educate the entire family about local history.

Getting Started on a Route 66 Trek

There is no better way to gain knowledge and perspective about the historical spots along California's Route 66 than to visit a Route 66 museum, such as those located in Victorville and Barstow in Southern California. Both offer extensive exhibits and displays that will heighten the excitement about touring the road and enjoying the sites firsthand.

Both museums boast gift shops featuring Route 66 memorabilia, maps and books. Donning a Route 66 T-shirt and hat add to the fun. Remember to slap the Route 66 shield on the car. En route to the Victorville museum, we always stop for breakfast at the historic Summit Inn, which is located at the summit of the Cajon Pass on Highway 15. Here westbound travelers would stop for a meal before winding through the historic gateway to San Bernardino and Southern California.

Later, we will visit many relics in the area, but for now we can enjoy a meal at the Summit Inn. Exiting Highway 15 at Oak Hill, you get that nostalgic twinge merely pulling into the parking lot, which is often filled with classic cars and motorcycles. The restaurant entrance has posted numerous articles evidencing its status as one of the Mother Road's remaining icons.

Patrons barely notice the lumpy booth seats, so enticed by the menu featuring such dishes as ostrich omelets and sausage. It is easy to get sucked into the retro atmosphere, knowing that the restaurant has served weary travelers since 1962. For years, our order was taken by waitress

Hilda Fish, a bee-hived, friendly lady with stories to tell. Sadly, she retired and is now deceased. Stop in the small gift shop on the way out.

Traveling north to Victorville, exit at D Street. The museum, established in 1995, is housed in a building that was once a Route 66 roadhouse, located between Fifth and Sixth Streets on Old Route 66. My favorite exhibit appears almost immediately as you enter. Donated by the Duarte Historical Society, this exhibit features the stick sign, Tiffany lamp and wagon wheel chandelier that once adorned the Trails Restaurant, a favorite steakhouse and lounge on Duarte's Route 66. Established in 1952, it was demolished in 2001. A stone plaque recognizing its iconic status is all that remains in its hometown.

Among the many exhibits featured is a favorite of museum visitors, Hula Ville, which is touted as "an example of unique roadside attractions once found all along the Mother Road." Miles Mahan, a retired carnival worker and poet, purchased a plot of land on Old Route 66 and displayed roadside litter on tree branches. He piqued the interest of passersby when he recycled a large discarded metal sign of a hula girl. That is when those who visited began the tradition of donating items to the display. When Mahan was no longer able to care for his collection, it was donated to the Route 66 museum.

Traveling on to Barstow, visiting the Mother Road Museum at 681 North First Street in the historic Harvey House, visitors are often greeted by full-time volunteer Debra Hodkin. Whether you peruse the exhibits on your own or ask for a narrated tour, you will learn about California's portion of Route 66. Here you can see the large metal sign that once topped the Blvd. Café, a famous eatery on Duarte's stretch of Route 66. The gift shop is extensive and the displays numerous. Admission to both museums is free. After visiting these museums, you are ready to explore the many places of interest along the Mother Road. Next, we will see the famed sites visited by westward-bound travelers as they finally crossed the California border. You may find that there is a lot more to see in Needles than you ever realized.

Part II
Needles to Barstow

Needles: Gateway to California

The year was 1938 when Alan J. Staller stepped onto the shoulder of Route 66 in Kansas City and stuck out his thumb. After days of hitchhiking, he finally reached the dusty border of California at Needles, anxious to continue on to Arcadia, where the Santa Anita racetrack was hiring workers.

"Hey buddy, you got a job?" demanded a deputy at the border, which at that time was controlled by the Los Angeles City Police Department, the closest law enforcement agency with enough staff for the job. Staller had to admit that he did not actually have a job but was confident that he would get one. The deputy told Staller to turn around and go home because there were already too many unemployed men in Southern California. His dreams dashed, he hitched back home.

A year later, Staller landed a job at the racetrack and once again thrust out his thumb, this time successfully crossing the border and ultimately settling in Monrovia. Later, his wife and two-year-old son, Bruce, boarded "The Scout," which Bruce called "the lowest of all trains." His father's colorful Route 66 stories, such as the one above, have remained vivid in Bruce's memory throughout the years. As a longtime resident of Monrovia and now Duarte, Bruce continues to live near the road that brought his family west.

Frustration and trepidation were two emotions shared by those who traveled on Route 66 in those days. If they were allowed to enter California,

In 1938, after hitchhiking from Kansas to the California border, Alan J. Staller was turned back by the authorities because he was unemployed. He later was allowed to pass after securing employment at the newly opened Santa Anita racetrack in Arcadia. *Courtesy of Bruce Staller.*

the difficult part had only begun. Searing summer temperatures plagued automobiles, which were not built to withstand severe heat. Traveling at night invited more obstacles, and gasoline stations were few and far between.

In 2001, we were fortunate to be among nine hundred people allowed to tour the El Garces Harvey House Hotel and Railroad Depot in Needles. A victim of vandals and the elements, this once bustling hotel and depot were an important part of Needles' history, and the 2001 tours were aimed at raising funds for renovation. The original depot, made of wood, was destroyed by fire in 1906, and the current concrete building was completed in 1908. It is named after a Spanish padre.

Passengers traveling through Needles on the Santa Fe Railroad could enjoy a brief stop at the depot and a hot meal expeditiously served by one of the Harvey Girls, who were young, lovely but modest and always cheerful. You can learn about the famed ladies by watching a 1946 movie called *The Harvey Girls*, starring Judy Garland and Angela Lansbury. Our tour of the depot was led by a former Harvey Girl who recalled colorful stories of the depot and the plight of the young ladies who left their homes to work in this desert outpost.

Subsequent visits to the depot have been disappointing, as the renovation project is moving at a snail's pace. However, the Friends of El Garces are determined to raise money to restore this Route 66 icon to its former splendor.

Across the street from the depot stands the Needles Regional Museum, a good place to learn about the area's history. Needles, named for its backdrop of pointed peaks, boasts a rich history, including that of the Mohave Indians, ranchers and hunters, as a gateway to California for Route 66 travelers.

Noah Jameson's Trip of Wonder

At the mention of the words "Route 66," a flood of memories envelops Noah Jameson. Raised in Joplin, America Highway's last stop in Missouri, he has lived his life within a stone's throw of the route. As a longtime resident of Duarte, and now living in La Verne with his wife, Rosemary, he has experienced the route's western end. Over the years, he has enjoyed trekking the road many times between Chicago and Santa Monica.

It was the summer of 1940 when Noah, age six, and his sister, Mary, age eleven, traveled Route 66 from Joplin to Ontario, California, on a Greyhound bus. "We sat up front behind the driver because of our ages," he recalls. "And when we were informed that we would be traveling through Indian territory, my childish thoughts turned to a story about 'Custer's Last Stand,' and I feared I would be losing my hair." He adds that "it wasn't until years later that I actually did lose my hair!"

Noah describes it as a "trip of wonder," recalling his excitement peering through the bus window catching glimpses of the Painted Desert and all the places that sold petrified wood. "We saw two-headed rattlesnakes, some real and some not-so-real, and we passed Indian teepee motels and giant arrows stuck in the ground. At the age of six, the sites along Route 66 were more wonderful than you could imagine."

The year Noah and Mary traversed Route 66 bound for California, the premiere of the motion picture adaptation of John Steinbeck's historic novel *The Grapes of Wrath*, under the direction of John Ford, was held.

Not to stray far from the Mother Road, Noah's home in La Verne is situated near several remnants of the days when Route 66 beckoned travelers west. Founded in 1887 by Isaac W. Lord, La Verne was originally dubbed "Lordsburg." The founder's dreams of success were soon dashed, and he sold his holdings to the German Baptist Brethren Church, which in turn established Lordsburg College, later to become the University of La Verne. In 1906, the town was incorporated, and the name changed to La Verne.

Consistent with the history of the famed route, La Verne joined in the frenzy of opening establishments to offer overnight accommodations and home-cooked meals to Route 66 travelers trekking through the town's boundaries. Surprisingly, a few of those establishments remain viable today, such as the La Paloma Restaurant, which has been serving Mother Road travelers since 1966.

"I've traveled Route 66 between Chicago and Santa Monica many times, both as a child and as an adult," says Jameson. "There are good memories, and some bad ones, but I do recall them all fondly."

GOFFS: A TREASURE IN THE DESERT

Goffs is an extremely important Route 66 town, despite the fact that it has been expelled from the famous highway. On our Route 66 trip, we leave the California border town of Needles and head for my personal favorite. At first glance, there is little remaining of the town of Goffs until you drive under the sign that reads "Study the Past." On the other side, you emerge into a different world to find a treasure that is under the tender care of the Mojave Desert Heritage and Cultural Association (MDHCA).

The Friends of the Old Mojave Road is an organization aimed at preserving a 138-mile trail once traversed by pioneers. This road was abandoned when railroads and more modern roads displaced it. Today, the Mojave Road winds through the East Mojave Preserve in much the same dusty, bumpy and sometimes barely passable condition as it did in the 1860s.

Above: The 1914 Goffs schoolhouse, once in ruins, has been restored and now houses a museum. Nearby is the town's library in which thousands of oral histories are stored.

Right: Drive under the sign and you pass into history at Goffs. Once located on Route 66, the town was later bypassed due to a realignment.

This hardscrabble main east–west route was displaced when the Santa Fe Railway was built. Goffs was a valuable stop where steam engines could replenish their water supply. The National Old Trails Road (also called the Ocean-to-Ocean Highway) was established in 1912, and in 1926, it was designated as the first national highway system for automobiles and renamed Route 66. Several years later, Route 66 was realigned to bypass Goffs when an eight-mile shortcut was carved through the Piute Mountains, skipping Goffs altogether.

Abandoned, Goffs' main landmark, a 1914 mission-style schoolhouse, fell into disrepair. As fate would have it, a lone man with a vision, Dennis Casebier, set out to save Goffs and recapture its fading history. Today, the MDHCA, under Casebier's direction, has renovated the schoolhouse to its former glory and established a museum within its walls. It was placed on the National Register of Historic Places by the federal government.

This aerial photograph was taken of Goffs in 2008. The town is now a living museum thanks to the efforts of Dennis Casebier and the Mojave Desert Heritage and Cultural Association.

Unlike many Route 66 towns in the area, Goffs is not waning—quite the contrary, in fact. A recent addition to the Cultural Center is the library, a replica of the historic Goffs Santa Fe Railway Depot (1902–1956). Within its walls is the massive Mojave Desert Archives. "There is no assemblage anywhere of material relating to the history of the Mojave Desert like the collections that exist at Goffs," says Casebier.

Visitors to the seventy-five-acre Goffs Cultural Center will find hundreds of artifacts rescued from the area's rich history, such as an Atlantic & Pacific Railway boxcar, a small courthouse that served the Amboy-Ludlow Judicial District in the 1940s, a Fraser-Chalmers ten-stamp mill, a Gilmore gasoline pump and a miner's cannon subject to a variety of claims regarding its origin.

Visitors are welcome at the Cultural Center on certain days or by appointment.

Plaques: Courtesy of E Clampus Vitus

E Clampus Vitus. Just the sound of it is intimidating, conjuring up visions of a horrible disease or perhaps a fraternity of enlightened scientists. Neither apply. It is a men's organization with dual personalities. Some "Clampers" call it a historical drinking society, while others dub it a drinking historical society. The members wear red shirts and funny hats. Whatever its secret purpose, it is a name you will find all along California's Route 66. If you see a historical plaque along the Route, it was probably the work of ECV.

One of the plaques recently erected on the Mother Road is located on the Veterans of Foreign Wars (VFW) building on Route 66 (Huntington Drive) and Santa Anita Avenue in Arcadia. It is dedicated to the U.S. Army Balloon School, which was built in 1918 and served as the training grounds for cadets learning to observe enemy activity from hot-air balloons. During construction, the workers lived in Lucky Baldwin's racing horse stables.

The school trained sixty-man ground crews responsible for raising and lowering the balloons, as well as two-man observation crews. The site was questionable because balloons were often damaged by the fickle winds of the area, but the school remained viable until the end of World War I in 1919.

The Ancient and Honorable Order of E Clampus Vitus is a fraternal disorganization. Although the members portray themselves as a gang of fun-loving jokesters, the historical plaques they have erected throughout the West serve as valuable one-page history books.

The plaque was dedicated on September 6, 2008, by ECV Platrix Chapter No. 2, of the Ancient and Honorable Order of E Clampus Vitus and the Arcadia Elks Lodge No. 2025.

Not far from Route 66, on August 9, 2010, the Clampers dedicated a plaque honoring the Adams Pack Station located at Chantry Flats in Big Santa Anita Canyon. In 1936, J.P. Steele obtained a special permit to operate a pack station and store at Chantry Flat, an enterprise that flourished until the great floods of 1938 washed much of it away, along with two hundred cabins in the area. He sold what was left, and although the station changed hands several times, it continued to operate, making it the only remaining pack station in Southern California.

On August 13, 1995, the Clampers erected a plaque in Sierra Madre at Hermosa and Carter Avenues honoring the town's wisteria vine, "the world's largest blossoming plant."

On Route 66 in Daggett, near Barstow, you will find an ECV Billy Holcomb Chapter plaque dedicated to the Daggett Garage, which "began life in the 1880s at the borax town of Marion." The garage was later moved to Daggett, where it housed an auto repair shop on the National Old Trails Highway.

Plaques appear along Route 66 from Chicago to the "End of the Route" plaque in Santa Monica. We have these visionaries to thank for providing permanent historical notes that remain long after the remnant has decayed or disappeared. These one-page history books may be found along many roads, most notably on the Mother Road and its environs. Near where Santa Monica Boulevard dead-ends at Ocean Boulevard, a brass plaque marks the official end of Route 66 and refers to it as the Will Rogers Highway, one of the many names of the famed highway.

Fenner and Essex: Alphabet Towns

Fenner is a small town in the Mojave Desert located on the Old Route 66, expelled from the current Mother Road by virtue of a highway realignment, much the same way the town of Goffs was evicted.

Approaching Fenner, one is greeted by twenty-foot letters spelling "GAS." The letters are not the only enormous thing about the town. The fuel at Fenner is so expensive that management has placed a sign on the front door of the store asking patrons not to harass the employees about that fact, even jokingly. Of course, such a sign only encourages barbs to be exchanged, but all in good humor.

A small picnic area with a pond, statues and cement benches invites patrons to linger and visit the store, which features a variety of desert, UFO and Route 66 memorabilia. Fast food and home-cooked dishes are served in the store's dining area, which is graced with a large fish tank. Customers usually run first to the clean restrooms.

On this section of the Mother Road, railroad water stations and towns were named in alphabetical order, and Fenner sits in the middle—Amboy, Bristol, Cadiz, Danby, Essex, Fenner, Goffs, Homer, Ibis and Java is the string of towns testament to this fact.

Traveling west from Fenner on Route 66, the next stop is Essex. Once a bustling town, it historically offered tourists a choice of cafés, markets and all-important garages with on-duty mechanics.

Despite these amenities, the town was best known as a place where you could get a free drink. So scarce was water in the desert, the restaurants

In Essex, travelers along the route found that water was scarce. To the rescue was the Auto Club, which installed a water fountain with a shake shingle roof for the purpose of quenching the thirst of motorists and radiators. It stands next to the highway today, although it's a bit crooked.

charged for drinking and to fill radiators. To the rescue was the Auto Club of Southern California, which established a free drinking fountain built to resemble an old-fashioned wishing well. Sitting just yards off the highway, the fountain remains intact today, albeit a bit cockeyed and out of order! You can view it and take photos today while traversing in an air-conditioned modern automobile. In times past, travelers were not so fortunate. Near the fountain, remnants of the old store and garages remain in a ghost town strewn with old tires.

It was some twenty miles from Essex that Jack Mitchell discovered a unique limestone cavern in the Providence Mountains. It was his desire that the public would visit his find and enjoy a tour of the cave and the magnificent view of the valley from his hand-built home. To that end, he single-handedly carved a road out of the desert floor from his abode to the town of Essex. The story of Mitchell Caverns is a fascinating one, deserving of an entire chapter.

Notable along the highway in the area is the graffiti. Not the painted blight that plagues many modern cities today, but graffiti perhaps better described as "rock art." Along the road, hundreds of names and messages fashioned from rocks, bottles and cans may be seen. Probably one day a few teens spelled out their names in such fashion, and later travelers followed suit by pulling over and adding their two cents. The same phenomenon has cropped up along the road in the form of "shoe trees" or "boxer shorts trees," on which the items flutter in the desert wind, prompting passersby to pull over and snap photographs.

A Trip that Never Ended

They were the best of buddies, typical teens growing up in the same Los Angeles neighborhood. But World War II ended the innocent life, and of their group of a dozen friends, all but two enlisted.

Manny Avila chose the navy, while Dick Sproul headed out with the merchant marines. When their duties ended, they met up again back home, facing a lull in life. Free from their enlistment and not yet enrolled in college, they came up with a crazy idea: "Let's go see New York." They worked their way to the East Coast on an Army Transport Service freighter, allowing them to pocket their subsistence pay, and when they reached port in December 1946, they found themselves in luck.

"Here we were, a couple of nineteen-year-olds seeing the sights of New York that we had only read about or seen in the movies," recalls Dick. When the boys learned that Nat King Cole was performing at the Paramount Theater, they purchased tickets. Maneuvering themselves into the front row, they enjoyed an evening of Christmas songs since the holiday season was upon them. Then suddenly, Cole changed his tune and sang, "Get your kicks on Route 66." "Why not?" they simultaneously asked. "Why not buy a car and drive home on Route 66?"

The boys called home to have money from their savings wired to them. Only a "rag top" would do for this journey, so off they went in a newly purchased and very used 1939 Ford Delux convertible that they later learned was a rust bucket. "Being California boys, we knew nothing of rusting cars," says Dick. "Warm weather was in the forecast, and we were on our way." After visiting relatives in New Jersey and Detroit, the pair spent the night at a YMCA and then picked up Route 66 in Chicago. As they headed west the first day, "It was early morning, and we were singing 'Take the highway, it's the best on Route 66.'"

Soon the blue skies disappeared. A severe cold front had moved into the Midwest, and the pair was plagued with freezing conditions. "Unfortunately, the car heater didn't work," recalls Dick. "Even our peacoats could not suffice, so we bundled up with blankets and took turns driving and sleeping. We passed all the roadside sites, only stopping at cafés for a quick meal and at gas stations to fill the tank."

"Four lanes turned to two, the temperature kept dropping, and we noticed glass-like frost encapsulated the bushes along the road. Our singing began to fade." The storm followed the boys for the entire week. "We were running out of time and money and regretfully passed by inviting little cabins with neon vacancy signs. We pushed on: Oklahoma City; Albuquerque; Flagstaff, Arizona; and even in Arizona it did not warm up. We pushed on: Winona, Kingman, Barstow."

"Racing to get home by Christmas, we finally drove the rust bucket down the Cajon Pass and suddenly the stormy sky opened up to a clear blue, and we were happy to be back in the California sun," Dick recalls.

Now in their senior years, and with Dick living in another state, the two still remain buddies, talk to each other frequently by phone and more often than not reminisce about their "trip of a lifetime," motoring down Route 66 singing the words they learned from Nat King Cole.

These two young men dared to act spontaneously, and although their trip was fraught with bad weather and other obstacles, they were better for it in the end. To this day, they often recall the excitement and adventure of traveling the Mother Road.

DANBY AND GENERAL PATTON

Headed west on Route 66, with the "town" of Essex in our rearview mirror, we look ahead to Danby. There is precious little evidence that Danby was once a town that took pride in serving a multitude of motorists, with the noble aim of serving the needs of travelers and, of course, making a dime.

The eyes of motorists in the 1920s, '30s and '40s would often frantically focus on their gas and temperature gauges as they whispered a prayer for a town to appear around the next curve. Innovations like GPS, CDs, satellite radio, cellphones, air conditioning, cruise control, digital cameras, remote keys and steel-belted radials were unheard of.

Danby, born as a railroad stop, grew to provide vital services to travelers. Today, curious visitors might venture 1.7 miles on the Danby Road to explore remnants of a campsite utilized by the U.S. Army during General George S. Patton's World War II desert training program. Throughout the area, General Patton exposed his troops to the extreme desert climate, terrain and occasional dust storms to prepare them for a planned assault on Rommel's forces in North Africa. The project encompassed more than eighteen thousand square miles and trained more than 1 million troops.

Remnants of the training camps remain. However, to learn more about this monumental endeavor, one must venture off Route 66 and visit the General George S. Patton Memorial Museum at Chiriaco Summit on Interstate 10 some thirty miles east of Indio. Established in 1988 to honor all veterans, the museum has dedicated many exhibits to the desert training program, and several World War II tanks are on display

There was a time Cadiz Summit greeted motorists with cafés, cabins and a garage. Today, it is a pile of rubble with the added insult of graffiti.

in the yard. Photo displays and a short movie reveal camp conditions and challenges that the soldiers encountered in the Mojave Desert.

West of Danby is Cadiz Summit, once a small but popular desert outpost. Here, eastbound motorists must negotiate a slight grade, one that proved a challenge to cars in the past. In the shade of graffiti-covered walls, one can sift through the remains of a gas station, a café and tourist cabins.

History in this area is buried in the sand or, in some cases, in the memories of those who lived there or merely traveled through. Bent and weathered remains of once thriving enterprises remind us of the fleeting nature of success and of how fickle fate can be. As traffic on Route 66 increased, so did the businesses that supported this trend. When bigger, faster and better highways replaced the Mother Road, motorists abandoned the street that once welcomed them. Some towns survived and some disappeared.

FATHER AND SON BOND ON THE MOTHER ROAD

Frank Ayala, fifty-three, of Huntington Park, fondly recalls the day he stood on the corner in Winslow, Arizona, with his son Xavier Lopez-Ayala ("Xavy"), then eighteen. That was just one of the memorable highlights of their journey.

Traveling along America's Highway headed for Michigan, where Xavy was to begin his first semester at Aquinas College, Frank knew that the trip would allow him to enjoy several days of his son's company. At the outset, they agreed that each would choose a radio station for one hour and then switch. When the Eagles' "Take It Easy" played, they were singing along and suddenly realized that their trip would take them to Winslow. Reaching town, they stopped to snap a photo "standing on the corner in Winslow, Arizona."

"At one stop," Frank recalls, "Xavy struck up a conversation with a waiter who told him that traveling Route 66 with his father would be a memory he would always cherish. The kind man sent us off with extra food for our trip."

At times driving on Interstate 40, the father and son did take opportunities to hop on the Mother Highway. "We had already scoured

Xavier Lopez-Ayala ("Xavy") accompanied his father, Frank, on a father-son bonding experience along America's Highway. Xavy, then eighteen years old, was on his way to college. *Courtesy of Frank Ayala.*

the Cajon Pass in our younger days but did drive the Helendale Route out of Barstow and stopped in Ludlow to snap some photos," says Frank.

When they left home, Frank told his son that he could ask any question he wanted and that a truthful answer would be forthcoming. Later, as they pulled out of Needles in 111-degree heat, Xavy casually asked, "Where did you meet my mother?" Frank was shocked, not at the question but by the timing, because they were at that moment passing the exact spot where his folks had met.

"I was hauling alfalfa from Posten, Arizona, to Chino, California, and each time I passed through the inspection station on the Needles border, I would see her. I finally asked her to dinner. The rest is history. If he had asked the question one hundred or even ten miles down the road, it would not have been such a coincidence," says Frank.

A TOWN IN SHAMBLES AND A PORTABLE COURTHOUSE

Motoring west on "the highway that's the best," travelers routinely pull over at the site of the Route 66 desert town of Chambless. One would think that the name reflects its state: shambles. Located about halfway between Needles and Barstow, this town and its environs are favorites of photographers and Route 66 buffs. At present a ghost town, a walk around the site offers evidence of the once important role it played in greeting weary travelers, gassing up their cars and offering a bit of shade from the relentless searing rays of the sun. The sign on the market is faded, but the large letters are photographically enticing. The entrance is blocked to ward off vandals, but at one time soldiers from an army training center in the area found relief within those walls.

Built of handmade adobe bricks, the market remained cool during the summer months. The inactive gas station has lost its pumps, but one can visualize a line of automobiles awaiting service. Although the town was known as a productive stop for those needing service, it has been described as "never really a town, only a shady spot on the desert route."

Chambless, a town in shambles today, was once a haven for motorists seeking food, shelter and respite from the desert sun. A few of the buildings, including the store, stand today.

One of the most photographed signs on the route is that of the Roadrunner Retreat Restaurant. Each year, it deteriorates further, victim of the extreme natural elements of the desert.

The site was named for James Albert Chambless, who homesteaded there in about 1920 and operated the store and gas station. It was one of the several towns along the route that provided water towers to serve the Atchison, Topeka and Santa Fe Railway. Tourist cabins offered overnight facilities, certainly a service appreciated by motorists traveling with families.

A mile and a half west of Chambless is one of the most photographed icons along the route. The towering sign that reads "ROADRUNNER RETREAT RESTAURANT," braced against the deep blue desert sky, features a large rendering of the iconic desert bird. It was used in a Dodge television commercial in 1988. Next to the "Roys" sign in nearby Amboy, the Roadrunner sign is a favorite for photographers, although its brilliance has faded, thanks to the unrelenting forces of nature.

In addition to serving as a café, the Roadrunner at one time was the site of the Danby Courthouse. This eight- by ten-foot portable courthouse, located in the Route 66 town of Danby just east of Chambless, was "hauled from place to place if court needed to be held someplace other than Danby." At one time, it made its home at the Roadrunner but was later returned to Danby.

THE ROAD'S HISTORY: A PART OF THE FAMILY

Throughout his life, he wore many hats: a father of seven, a lawyer so creative that he was known to write pleadings in rhyme, an advocate of the working man, a judge, an avid Dodgers fan and, alas, an author. By default, Lewis Garrett became painfully familiar with California's Route 66 when he opened a law office in San Bernardino while residing in Hollywood with his family. He commuted on Route 66 daily, that being the obvious choice at the time.

Despite the demands of work and family, Garrett published several books, two of which contain valuable information for those researching extant or vanished Route 66 towns. Two of his writings, now out of print—*San Bernardino County Place Names* (self-published, 1996) and "The Postal History of San Bernardino County" (in the *San Bernardino County Museum Association Quarterly* 39, no. 4)—reflect years of research accomplished before computers. Hundreds of index cards with handwritten notes contain the results of face-to-face interviews with postmasters and postmistresses, many of whom had long since retired and are now deceased.

Entries, such as those below, list the names of the postmasters, some from the mid-1800s, and then set forth tidbits of the town's history garnered through postal records and personal interviews.

Lewis Garrett, man of many talents, spent years interviewing retired postmasters who once worked along Route 66. He authored several books on place names and postal history of the area.

- *Alta Loma: "When the Pacific Electric line planned to go through the area in 1913, residents were asked to choose a name for its station. Instead of Loamosa, which had been the community name since 1895, they selected Alta Loma as more fitting and euphonious."* [Post office established on December 21, 1903, rescinded and reestablished in 1904.]
- *Cucamonga: "Community established by the Cucamonga Colony on the old stage road between S.B. and L.A. At the time the P.O. started in 1864, Cucamonga (often spelled Cocomonga at that time) was an agricultural area with fruit trees and vineyards…The word Cucamonga is derived from an Indian word for 'sandy place.'"* [Post office established in March 1864, and the name was changed to Rancho Cucamonga in January 1986.]
- *Fontana: "A town named Rosena was planned at this site in 1887 but failed to develop. In 1913 the name Rosena was officially changed to Fontana by a vote of the residents. The community was a leading poultry and pig-raising area and in 1926 had 500 families in the poultry business."* [Post office established in August 1964.]
- *Upland: "The change of name from North Ontario was championed by resident Charles D. Adams, an early settler, who thought the name appropriate for its higher altitude and to free it from possible annexation by Ontario."* [Post office name changed from North Ontario in March 1902.]

These are a few examples of historical facts discovered through postal records and the recollections of past postmasters. On the cusp of his ninetieth birthday, Garrett is affectionately referred to as "the Judge" at Pasadena Highlands in Pasadena. Today, he barely recalls writing these books, and his mind blurs when I ask him about the days he commuted on Route 66.

In an effort to refresh his fading memory, I ask him about the postmasters he interviewed and the places he visited, but the interrogation confuses him and he becomes frustrated. Ashamed of my prodding, I kiss him on the forehead and tell him, "It's okay, Dad." Moments later, my father is peacefully sleeping.

A RESURRECTED TOWN AND THE JOKE OF THE CENTURY

It was a quiet morning in Amboy when the townspeople, to their horror, spotted smoke spiraling from the "dormant" crater southwest of town. Panic set in. Route 66 was shut down, as was the Santa Fe Railroad mainline. Residents could swear that the ground beneath them was shaking.

Hadn't they noticed the smiles on the faces of students from Barstow High School? Wasn't the date, April 1 (1945), a clue? According to the California Route 66 Association, the *Los Angeles Times* hired a media plane, a reporter and photographer to investigate, and soon the hoax was revealed. For months, the students had hauled trash and tires up the trail to the cinder cone, and on the fateful day, set it afire.

Amboy is a town that refuses to die, bucking the fate of its neighbors. Best known for its iconic sign advertising Roy's Café, this town has a population of about eight.

Arriving at Roy's, I am greeted by the town sheriff, Farrell Hastings. He points to where a fire station will soon be built and confirms that the

Thar she blows! Amboy Crater was the scene of one of the biggest jokes played out on the route. The town residents panicked when smoke began to spew from the crater and could swear that they felt the ground shaking.

Amboy sheriff Farrell Hastings takes responsibility for protecting the town. He is frequently on hand to greet visitors. The town has been purchased and is under restoration.

post office is open for business. Across the street is an old Volkswagen, which he says serves as a search and rescue vehicle.

The town is owned by Albert Okura, who also owns the Juan Pollo Restaurant chain and the first McDonald's restaurant site in San Bernardino, which he operates as a museum. Motorists may gas up at Roy's and drop into the café for Route 66 memorabilia and a personal greeting from the sheriff. "Wheels turn slowly around here," he says. "One day, the motel and café will be finished, and motorists can stop and stay a while."

The closed schoolhouse stands, as does the church, albeit a bit crooked. Clean restrooms are located behind the courtyard guarded by large statues of a ram and horse.

Amboy is located about an hour and a half west of Needles and east of Barstow. The nearby crater was designated as a national natural landmark in 1973, and a historical plaque was placed there by the Billy Holcomb Chapter of E Clampus Vitus at the parking area entrance. The crater is accessible by a 3.5-mile trail. A picnic area provided by the Needles Field Office offers covered picnic tables, restrooms and a 1.1-mile path to the crater trailhead. A viewing platform offers an amazing view of the crater, as well as the lava lakes, tubes, sinks and spatter cones beyond.

Amboy is fighting to stay on the map, not for the reasons that spurred its birth but rather as a bastion of nostalgia, an opportunity for the people of today to understand the plight of those who traveled the Mother Road in search of a new beginning.

Waving goodbye to Amboy, we head west toward Barstow to visit some forgotten towns that have vanished into the desert sand.

A RAILROAD WORKER'S DAUGHTER MOVES TOWN TO TOWN

Although service stations, cafés and motels served travelers along Route 66, that was not the only reason these communities survived. For many, the main purpose was to serve the railway system and provide water for the steam engines rumbling through. Migrant

Sue Ellen Willis and Bootsie take a rest on railroad ties. Sue Ellen's father, a railroad worker, moved his family from town to town along the tracks. Migrant railroad workers made up a portion of the population of towns along the route in the Mojave Desert. *Courtesy of Sue Ellen Willis.*

railroad workers maintaining and working on the tracks populated these small towns, often with their families in tow.

Sue Ellen Willis, a resident of Covina for forty-five years, fondly recalls her early years as the daughter of a railroad worker and the plight of her family moving along the tracks in the Mojave Desert.

In the 1940s, V.L. "Pete" Young worked as a supervisor for Silva & Hill Construction Company, shoring up the rail sidings for the troop trains crossing from camps to the West Coast.

"At that time, I was in the third grade, and as the work progressed, we would move from town to town. I remember all the towns between Needles and Barstow," says Sue Ellen. She attended schools in several towns along the route, including in Amboy and Essex. "Boy, what an education that was," she says. She remembers the trains stopping to load water from the towers and the time her father volunteered to take her entire class to the lava fields near Amboy.

Pete was a foreman, and "he liked nothing better than to run the equipment 'cats,'" says Sue Ellen. "I would tell my classmates that my dad was a cat skinner, and they would give me this funny look. Pete was always helping out travelers if they needed something, like a tire or loaf of bread." Sometimes, families would become stranded at the station, and he was happy to give them a hand. He was a proud member of the International Operating Engineers Union until his death in the early 1990s.

"When we left the desert, I was certainly glad to finally settle with my family in Alhambra and to finish the lower grades at one school and then on to high school. All and all, living on Route 66 in the railroad towns was an experience that I have never forgotten. I especially recall how my mother always kept me dressed with ribbons in my hair."

Towns and icons along the route, no matter their present shape, continue to evoke memories for those who traveled the road, whether five or fifty years ago. There is a mystic power that hovers above the asphalt, elevating Route 66 to a road more revered than highways that are newer, longer and arguably more scenic.

A study to survey California's Route 66 will soon commence, funded by the California Preservation Foundation in partnership with the National Park Service Route 66 Corridor Preservation Program. Its aim is to document historic sites along the road to determine which one will be nominated for a "slot in the National Register of Historic Places."

"Route 66 is a piece of roadside Americana that is like nothing else in the world," according to David Knudson, executive director of the National Historic Route 66 Federation.

A Lonely Patch of Desert Hides a Secret

Traveling along Route 66 heading west, we leave Amboy, the town that refuses to die, and pull over at the site of Bagdad, a lonely and eerie patch of desert, now home only to the deceased. Peering out over the parched land, a strange feeling overcomes me. I see no cars on Route 66 ahead or behind. All around me there is an unsettling stillness, a vast emptiness.

Peering out over the desert, I see only shrubs, gravel and railroad tracks. There is a lone tree, a forlorn sentinel silently guarding the parched earth where Bagdad once thrived. Some guidebooks describe a second tree, a palm, which also marked the site, but it is nowhere to be seen. It is hard to believe that here a small desert camp blossomed into the largest

The hidden cemetery of Bagdad has received continuous grooming and restoration by an anonymous good Samaritan who has taken it upon himself to add dignity to the previously untended graves.

community between Daggett and Needles by 1910. Established in 1883 as a siding on the Southern Pacific Railroad, it later housed a Santa Fe station, a school, a church and a Harvey House, which was distinctive because it employed men instead of the famed "Harvey Girls." Bagdad was the headquarters for the Orange Blossom Mine.

Because of the similarity in temperature, this vanished town was named after the Iraq city of Baghdad, with a tweak in the spelling. Bagdad is said to be the driest spot in North America, and between 1912 and 1914, there was no rain for 767 consecutive days. Yet Bagdad had an ample supply of water, a rare commodity in the desert.

The hub of major mining traffic, a main dirt road from town led south to the Dale mining district and on another branch to Twentynine Palms. In the early 1900s, the town began to fade as travelers abandoned the Dale–Twentynine Palms Road with its inherent hazards and chose to travel on a graded road out of nearby Amboy.

Bagdad was a major gold shipping point. A stage line carried passengers and freight between the depot and the Orange Blossom Mine. By 1903, gold mining in the area had almost ended. The post office was closed, and only a few buildings, a café and a gas station remained. The town was razed in 1958.

Suddenly, a roar shatters the stillness around me. A rumble and a whistle—a train! I watch it ramble along like a giant snake, and after it passes I notice something strange on the north side of the tracks. Scrambling up the berm and across the tracks, I stumble upon a small cemetery. Surrounded by a flimsy wire, sun-baked rocks outline the graves, each marked with a simple wooden cross. Someone has neatly raked the area, but mysteriously, not one shoeprint mars the lines. There are no names or telltale marks, but here lie those who presumably inhabited the town of Bagdad, and here they remain—unnamed, unmarked and likely forgotten by all but a few.

Several miles west of Bagdad is the site of Siberia, named by the Southern Pacific Railway when the original line was built. After the Santa Fe took over, the name was retained. This was never really a town but rather a siding that was opened in 1883 to handle tonnage from the salt mines on Bristol Lake. Later Leslie Salt Company harvested thirty thousand tons of salt and a like amount of calcium chloride annually from the site.

That's enough of the dead and dying towns of the Mojave; its time for a hearty lunch at the Ludlow Café. Heading west, we will soon reach Ludlow, where serving travelers is still a priority.

Note: After the above segment was published, I received a kind e-mail from someone who wished to remain anonymous. He told me of a stop he made at the Bagdad site while headed east on business. He came upon the cemetery, which was the victim of vandals and the elements. The crosses and markers were strewn about. Maintenance of the graveyard became his personal challenge, and since that time he has returned time and again, raking, replacing the stones and mending the crosses. I was so impressed by his dedication to the cemetery that on my next visit to the area I placed flowers on the grave sites.

Obstacles and Milestones Evoke Memories

Whether it be difficult times, such as digging out the car on washed-out portions of the road, or milestone events such as spending a wedding night in a wigwam, memories of Route 66 linger in the minds of many long after their journey ended.

Kenneth Pitzer

"We would always carry a pick and shovel when traveling by car in those days," says Kenneth Pitzer, eighty-eight, who has resided in Arcadia since 1984. He was only a year old when his folks brought the family from Kansas to Northern California on Route 66. "My father was an adventurer and headed west because he had visions of a land of opportunity. He took our family to live among the vineyards for a time."

In 1930, his mom and dad loaded Kenneth and his five siblings into their 1928 Chevy and headed back to Oklahoma and Kansas, pulling a two-wheel trailer.

"When Route 66 was dedicated in 1926, they merely put up road signs on the highway just as it was. Much of the route was grated dirt road, and travelers had to fend for themselves in the case of a washout or other obstructions. On that trip, more than once we had to get out and dig," he recalls. There were times when the car couldn't make it over a hill with the weight of the trailer.

The trip took about a week, with a short stay in Flagstaff, where his mother could do laundry. When they reached Oklahoma, the cost of gas was about six cents per gallon. "My father didn't like to stay in one place too long," he remembers. As a young man, Pitzer returned to California and married Charlotte. They recently celebrated their forty-fifth wedding anniversary.

Lonell and Marguerite Spencer

It was in January 1951 when Lonell Spencer of Arcadia and Marguerite Williams, born and raised in Monrovia, married at the Church of the Good Shepherd. Following the reception, the couple headed east on Route 66 for their honeymoon. Marguerite didn't know what to think when Lonell pulled up at the Wigwam Motel in Rialto and registered.

Lonell and Marguerite Spencer were married in Arcadia in 1951 at the Church of the Good Shepherd, after which they took to the Mother Road and headed east. *Courtesy of the Spencers.*

WIGWAM VILLAGE NO. 7
2728 Foothill Blvd.
SAN BERNARDINO, CALIF.

WIGWAM No.	DATE	AMT. PAID	CLERK
11	1-19-51	$ 5.00	[illegible]

GUESTS NOT CHECKING OUT BY 12:00 NOON WILL BE CHARGED FOR ANOTHER DAY. GUESTS STAYING OVER PLEASE NOTIFY THE OFFICE. THE MANAGEMENT ASSUMES NO RESPONSIBILITY FOR INJURY OR LOSS OF ANY KIND.

Marguerite Spencer was surprised when they reached the Wigwam Motel in Rialto, where her husband carried her over the threshold. To this day, she keeps in her bride book the five-dollar receipt for the evening's lodging.

"I liked it because it was level and easy to carry her over the threshold," says Lonell, now eighty-one. "When I told them in the office that we were just married, their response was, 'Yes, we can tell.'"

They recall exactly how much that night at the Wigwam cost: a whopping five dollars. "We know," says Lonell, "because she still has the receipt in her bride's book!"

Lonell was no stranger to California's stretch of the Mother Road. His folks owned a cabin in Crestline, so he would take the route often. "It was a wide-open highway back then, and I remember speeding along at about seventy miles per hour with citrus orchards on both sides of the road."

"Things were a lot different," he says, recalling a time when he and his buddies were headed for the snow in his mother's Plymouth. Suddenly, there was a problem with a wheel, and they could drive no farther. Pulling over with little but country around them, they took off on foot, finding a house nearby. A man was in his garage working on his roadster, and when they told him of their woes, he grabbed his tools and some parts and was able to fix the wheel. He turned down the money they offered and said he'd be paid back if they would just help out someone else in need some day.

Ludlow: The Town that Moved

The gas stations, eateries and minimarket of the Route 66 town of Ludlow are located just a hair off I-40 some thirty-six miles east of Barstow. The town serves travelers today just as it did in the 1940s, and this is no accident.

Ludlow was named for William C. Ludlow, railroad master car repairer. In the early 1880s, it served as a water stop for steam engines. In the 1900s, Ludlow was served by three railroads: the Santa Fe, the Tonopah and Tidewater and the Ludlow-Southern Railroad, which carried ore from the Bagdad-Chase mine ten miles south of town. The mine superintendent, it is said, declared it a "closed camp," banning liquor and women, which only encouraged the vice-intentioned clientele to set up shop in nearby Ludlow.

In 1913, Ludlow consisted of two businesses, two general stores, three cafés, a pool hall, a barbershop, two rooming houses, a post office, a Standard Oil Company office, a rail station, the railroad and homes. Water was brought in from the town of Newberry Springs by railcar. The town was, by all accounts, a lively one and was looking at a rosy future.

However, success can be elusive, and when the steam engines were replaced by diesel and the ore deposits petered out, hope for growth and prosperity waned. The final hit came when I-40 replaced Route 66—tourism practically ceased, leaving the town high and dry.

Then the resourceful Ludlowians, if I may dub them us such, picked up town and moved it closer to the offending highway, thereby guaranteeing continued success. For that reason, it remains a busy little "town" where travelers may gas up, use the restroom and buy munchies for the trip ahead.

Today's travelers can recapture a feel of the Old Route 66 days when they eat at the Ludlow Café. The food portions are hearty, and at a recent visit, we were served by a curt waitress who had just finished bawling out the staff within earshot of the customers. The café offers a sheet of paper with a list of facts about the town:

> *Until 1988 the telephones had no dials and you waited for the operator in San Bernardino or Los Angeles to pick up the line to place a call out.*

When calling into Ludlow an operator was needed to ring into the phone numbers which were Ludlow #1, #2, #3, etc....Each location had to listen for distinctive rings to identify which business they were ringing for.

There are remnants of old town buildings, a gas station and hotels, all of which attract photographers from near and far. Rockhounds also visit the area to rummage through the many gem fields within a twenty-mile radius of town.

TRAVELING THE ROAD WITH SHORTS AND SOCKS

Three teens in a roadster took to the Mother Road more than sixty years ago, and the experience remains vivid in their memories, reminding them of those innocent years when that sort of freedom was reserved for the young.

Fred Johnson, a resident of Covina for forty-five years, shared his story in such a poignant manner that it is best told in his own words:

In 1947 at the age of seventeen, Fred Johnson accompanied his friend Bill on a Route 66 trek in Bill's 1930 Ford roadster. All he packed was a clean pair of sox and shorts. *Courtesy of Fred Johnson.*

Back in 1947, at the age of seventeen, and not familiar with any part of the country but Los Angeles where I was raised, I had an opportunity to go on this trip. You see, one of my buddies named Bill was from Deming, New Mexico, wanted to return there to visit family and asked me to go along. Another buddy, also named Bill, joined us.

Back then, most of the guys had hot rods, and Bill was no exception. He had a 1930 Ford roadster with a Ford flat-head engine, no fenders, no top and no hood. Nowadays, it would be called a "rat rod."

My knowledge of traveling was nil, and my entire wardrobe for the trip was a clean pair of sox and a pair of shorts.

The three of us in the hot rod headed east, and when we got to Pomona, the car stopped running. The culprit was a bad coil, so we found a parts house and soon we were on the road again. By the time we got to Phoenix (thanks, Glenn Campbell), the sun was coming up, and it was getting hot driving through the desert.

To stay awake, we stopped at every wigwam and hot dog joint along the way for pie and coffee, which was all we could afford. My girlfriend, Dawn, now my wife of sixty-one years, baked us cookies to eat along the way.

Today, Fred Johnson has his own hot rod, a bright red 1929 Ford roadster. *Courtesy of Fred Johnson.*

Well, the hot rod and the three of us made it to Deming. Back then, Deming had one stop sign in the middle of town, and all the side streets were dirt. When we left Deming, we headed south to Columbus, New Mexico, to get a little history on Pancho Villa.

Let me tell you, that day was really hot. About halfway to Columbus, in a field there was a well that pumped water into a big tank. The water ran over the top of the tank so the cattle could have water to drink. Well, you guessed it! We stopped, ran over, took off our clothes and jumped in. Man did that feel good! Not to worry, there was no one around in the middle of nowhere. Looking back, that was a lot of fun. I think the cattle thought we were a little crazy. After visiting El Paso and Carlsbad Caverns, we were back on Route 66 and drove straight home. All three of us were hot, tired and sleepy, but Route 66 got us home.

This was an adventure we will never forget. Now that I am older, Bill and I still talk and laugh about our kicks on Route 66.

Today, I have my own hot rod, a 1929 Ford roadster with a big block Chevy motor, and oh yes, it has a top, fenders and hood. On some Saturday mornings, my wife and I cruise Route 66. We even stop and have pie and coffee. Some things you just love to do at any age.

His story helps to explain why Route 66 is more than a road. It has powers beyond a mere highway, reminding oldsters that they were once youngsters.

NEWBERRY SPRINGS: A CAVE, A CRATER AND A CULT FILM

A cave, a crater and a ragtag café of movie fame are strange bedfellows on a stretch of the Mother Road in the western portion of the Mojave Desert. They are on or near Route 66 in the vicinity of the often-overlooked town of Newberry Springs.

Atop an ancient lake, Newberry Springs, once known as Warm Springs, enjoys a high water table, which made it an ideal water stop for steam-powered trains. The Southern Pacific set up a station there in 1883. The town's supply of water was so ample that it exported water via tank cars to "dry towns" in the area.

So rich with water is Newberry Springs that in the past, and even today, water seeps into excavated areas, creating small lakes and ponds for recreation and irrigation.

Newberry Cave, located in the Newberry Mountains, is a draw to adventurers and archaeologists. Also called the Schuilling Cave, it requires a short hike into a steep canyon. Here archaeological items have been unearthed that suggest that cultural activities took place at the site as far back as 1500 BC.

On the short ride west from Ludlow to Newberry Springs, a prominent sight will catch your eye. The looming black Pisgah crater is a young volcanic cinder cone that may have been active twenty thousand years ago. Although the land surrounding the crater is privately owned and subject to aggregate mining, it is a favorite spot of spelunkers, who relish in navigating through miles of lava tubes and tunnels.

This desert town has another claim to fame. The Sidewinder Café in Newberry Springs is the site where the cult movie *Bagdad Café* was filmed in 1987. That name stuck after the movie became popular. The original

The Sidewinder Café in Newberry Springs was renamed the Bagdad Café for the filming of what became a cult movie. The restaurant staff acted in the movie alongside the film's star, Jack Palance.

Bagdad Café was located in the now vanished town of Bagdad, east of Newberry Springs.

"The original movie title was *Out of Rosenheim*," according to Linda Lee of Monterey Park, a dedicated fan of the movie. "I remember reading that it was a big hit in Germany, and tourists come to the U.S. just to visit it." In the loose plot, a Bavarian couple touring the California desert become stranded when the car breaks down. After an argument, the wife, Mariane Sagebrecht, luggage in tow, stomps off and ends up at the café, where she befriends the odd characters at the fleabag truck stop.

The real characters at the café appeared as extras and during filming hung out with the film's stars, including Jack Palance. Belly up to the counter today, and the staff will dish out an earful, pointing out the movie photos and memorabilia that decorate the walls. The film's success was followed by a short-lived TV sitcom starring Whoopi Goldberg and Jean Stapleton.

The café is located about one hundred miles from the San Gabriel Valley, a bit far for lunch but worth the experience. Out of Barstow on I-40, it is located just off the Newberry Springs exit on the National Trails Highway. Don't expect a gourmet meal, but you are sure to get an earful of Route 66 nostalgia, memorable photos and an autograph.

THE SWEET FRAGRANCE OF CITRUS LINGERS

Vanished cafés, the fragrance of citrus sifting through prolific orchards and the satisfying gulp of freshly squeezed orange juice from a stand along the Mother Road—these are among the memories that linger for those who traveled along Route 66 in the San Gabriel Valley.

Joy French-Paris

When she travels on Huntington Drive in Arcadia these days, a particular Route 66 memory captures Joy French. It was in July 1954, when a mutual friend introduced her to Ron Paris at Carpenters, a café once famous for its shrimp and fried chicken.

Ron and Joy's first date was to the county fair in Pomona, and they married that December. The two recently celebrated their fifty-fifth wedding anniversary. When a lady named Joy French marries a man named Ron Paris, well, that is a story in itself!

Joy has resided in Temple City since 1935, "but I went to El Monte Schools because there was no high school in Temple City," she recalls. The couple has raised three daughters. "Unfortunately, Carpenters has been demolished, but the good memories return when I drive in the area of the racetrack and see the current 100-to-1 Club." She also has fond memories of traveling with her folks on Route 66 when she was a child, headed to the local mountains "and passing little stone houses with stands selling orange juice."

Don Pascoe

Give Don Pascoe, seventy-seven, a whiff of orange blossoms, and his mind drifts back to the days when, as a ten-year-old, his folks loaded him and his twin brother, Ron, into the family Oldsmobile and traveled on Route 66 from West Hollywood to Cousin Dorothy's house in La Verne.

"It was such a long drive from West Hollywood to La Verne," he recalls, "that we had to stay the night and come home the next day." But Don didn't mind because Cousin Dorothy owned a roadster, and she would run them up to the snow at Mount Baldy, an experience still fond in his memory. Today, Dorothy Doyen remains in La Verne, and Don resides in Covina. Besides the sweet, permeating fragrance of orange blossoms, Don remembers seeing smudge pots in the orchards, as well as many orange stands along the way. "You could buy a crate of oranges or a fresh-squeezed cup of orange juice."

Charlotte Plunkett

"I've lived in the same house in Glendora for fifty-seven years," says Charlotte Plunkett, who recalls many trips on Route 66 when she was a child. Her sister moved to Los Angeles, and to keep in personal touch, her mother would drive the family from Iowa to Los Angeles to visit. Eventually, they moved to Glendora.

"I loved Glendora because it was country," she says, "but oh how we loved to see the lights when we would catch the Red Car into Los Angeles."

Orange juice stands were all the rage in the 1940s, but precious few remain. Some juice stands added food to their limited menu and eventually morphed into restaurants. Walt Wiley's Drive-In, located at Grand Avenue and Alosta in Glendora, featured fresh OJ, eventually carrying on as the Hickory Inn before it joined the list of long lost Route 66 icons.

Daggett: A Parade of Colorful Characters

Although the Mojave Route 66 town of Daggett shares a common history with neighboring communities, it has many claims of distinction, such as the colorful characters that were familiar faces around town.

The naturalist John Muir was a frequent visitor in the dusty desert town of Daggett. He came to visit his daughter, Helen, who had moved to Daggett for health reasons. He was known to stay at the Stone Hotel, which was built in 1875. It stands today and is rumored to be the subject

Despite rumors of a pending restoration project, the 1875 Stone Hotel in Daggett seems to be crumbling. Here is where John Muir visited his daughter and where Death Valley Scotty and Shorty Harris planned their questionable mining operations.

of future renovation. In 1914, Muir suffered his final illness in Daggett and died a few days later in Los Angeles.

Muir was not the only popular name to frequent the Stone Hotel. Here Death Valley Scotty and Shorty Harris planned their mining operations and questionable deals. It is said that racing legend Barney Oldfield sped through Daggett in a desert race, and some say Wyatt Earp visited more than once.

At one time, the town's reputation was described as a "lurid hotbed of vice." It is rumored that this may have been attributed to a shootout at Alex's Bar, where a man was killed. Thereafter the bar was known as the Bucket of Blood. Daggett boasts a colorful history with an intriguing railroad backdrop. Today, it looks like a town that doesn't know whether to improve or give up. Dilapidated homes, lots strewn with junk and structures melting to earth are in sharp contrast with recreational parks and a museum in midtown. It is the location of the Barstow-Daggett Airport and a solar energy facility.

Located just ten miles from Barstow, Daggett gets lost in the big picture. Circa 1882, "Daggett was called 'Calico' because it housed a depot off what was then the Southern Pacific Railroad mainline, the closest depot to the town site of Calico. In 1883, to avoid confusion, the name was changed to Daggett," according to railroad buff Larry Boerio.

The town's namesake, John R. Daggett, was California's lieutenant governor from 1883 to 1887. He was also owner of the Bismark Mines in Calico. Daggett was originally a town for miners and a supply center. It was the terminus of the Borate and Daggett eleven-mile rail line and the four-mile industrial Columbia Mine Railway. By all accounts, it was destined to become a major town before it was eclipsed by Barstow.

Today, there are historical spots where one can take photos and perhaps capture the essence of the town's better days. Splendid abodes of the past are withered but make for great photography. The Stone Hotel still stands, and nearby is a photographer's prize, Fout's Garage, originally used as a roundhouse for narrow-gauge railroad equipment. It was operated by Waterloo Mill and Mining Company to haul ore from Calico.

Also nearby is the California Agricultural Station, as was described on its sign, but history notes that it was manned by the authorities who, at one time, systematically turned back migrants who had no job or money. The station was enlarged in 1953 by building onto the front of the original station. It is abandoned but is said to be the last standing migrant control station.

MEGGINSON: FIVE HUNDRED MILES A DAY

Bob Megginson was just thirteen years of age when his father loaded the family into their 1936 Chevrolet sedan at three o'clock in the morning and hopped onto Route 66 in San Bernardino, headed for New Castle, Delaware, a small town just south of Philadelphia, Pennsylvania. His mother and father were originally from New Castle and were looking forward to a family reunion.

"We got as far as the outskirts of Needles when we lost a timing gear and had to spend most of the next day getting it fixed," says Bob. "We sat in the heat of the day outside the small garage."

Stopping at iconic Route 66 spots was not an option for the Megginson family because the father was determined to travel five hundred miles a day. "That was no small task since every day we encountered detours and road construction," Bob recalls. "At night, we would stay in small cabins called motor lodges, but we would not stop until we hit the five-hundred-mile mark, even if it meant passing a nice place to stay." He recalls that one of the overnight spots was in the home of a stranger.

The evening stop was usually at about 8:00 p.m., and the family would be on the road by 5:00 a.m. the next morning. At times, they would eat at small cafés and diners. "Eating was always an adventure. There were no McDonald's or Subways, only family-owned diners with local favorite dishes." For lunch, Bob and his sister, Dorothy Ann, then eleven, would eat sandwiches their mother had packed.

Despite the five-hundred-mile edict, Bob remembers many sites along the way. "Route 66 was a two-lane asphalt highway with spells of dusty dirt washboard detours. I remember the Burma-Shave signs and the small cabins where we stayed. Once a car in front of us hit a skunk, and we suffered from the smell for two days."

Bob remembers lightning bugs in Missouri, how hot it got in the middle of the day and how they drove across the Arizona and

California desert at night to avoid the heat. "I remember the Indians in Arizona selling jewelry and blankets along the road."

"You have to remember that before the war in 1941, there was very little travel across the country, as the roads and vehicles were not made for long-distance travel," Bob says. "So when we got to New Castle, we received a warm welcome as the first 'travelers' in our family."

On the way home, the Megginsons were on Route 66 in Missouri when "we broke a rod in the engine and limped into a small town." They went to the only garage for help, but the owner/mechanic said that there had been a flood and he was rebuilding tractors and had no time to fix the Chevrolet. "However, he did give us a corner of his garage and let my dad and I use his tools so we could repair the car ourselves." After two days, the car was running, and the family headed home. "The owner wouldn't accept payment; he just wished us good luck."

A resident of West Covina since 1959, Bob, now seventy-five years old, vividly remembers the sites.

Part III
Barstow to San Bernardino

Barstow: Where Many Paths Cross

Motorists who stop in Barstow for gas and then head out have missed one of the largest and most historic of the California Route 66 towns. Barstow's main street is Route 66, which the town proudly labels the "Main Street of America." Historically, Barstow served as a major transportation hub in the desert, first with foot trails, followed by railroads, Route 66 and then major highways. It is the site where many paths cross. Today, two major interstates (Interstate 15 and Interstate 40) meet in Barstow. In times past, it was the convergence of the Old Mojave Road, the Old Mormon Trail and the National Trails Highway, later Route 66. Railroad tracks linked passengers to the north, south, east and west.

In 1882, when silver was discovered in Calico, six miles north of Barstow, the town began to thrive. Its success was ensured when the Santa Fe Railway arrived. Today, you can stand near the tracks at the depot and with a little imagination hear the roar of the trains and the flurry of rushing passengers. The rail station is on the National Register of Historic Places (listed in 1975). Named the Casa del Desierto, it was rebuilt in 1911 by the Fred Harvey Company after the original depot burned down. In the new Harvey House, railway passengers could indulge in gourmet meals served by the famed Harvey Girls.

The Casa del Desierto rail station in Barstow is on the National Register of Historic Places. The building, which housed a Harvey House, has been restored.

Sadly, the Casa eventually fell into disrepair, a victim of vandals and the elements. When the Santa Fe Railway announced plans to tear it down, many local historians and architects rallied to save it. Today, it has been rebuilt and houses the Greyhound and Amtrak stations, several arts groups, the chamber of commerce and two museums.

There are a number of "must see" spots for Route 66 buffs to visit in Barstow. The famous El Rancho Motel, built with railroad ties from the defunct Tonopah and Tidewater Railroad, may soon reopen, and a meal at the classic El Rancho Café is a must. While a great many plastic fast-food establishments compete for your attention, there are historic gems among them that are easily missed.

Route 66 buffs could spend hours at the California Route 66 Mother Road Museum, located at the depot, which features among the extensive exhibits the sign from the Blvd. Café, a Route 66 icon that was located in Duarte. Also at the depot is the Western America Railroad Museum. The nearby Mojave River Valley Museum offers myriad exhibits, while the Desert Discovery Center, located in a field office of the Bureau of Land Management, has on display the "Old Woman Meteorite," the second-largest meteorite in the United States.

The McDonald's Barstow station is probably the most unique of the chain, as patrons can eat a Big Mac in a train car. And when traveling through Barstow, stop and peruse the numerous murals that offer historic artistic comment on the local history.

Dries Bessels: Route 66 via Amsterdam

What would possess a person from the Netherlands to embrace the mystic qualities of America's Main Street? Dries Bessels, forty-nine, lives in Amsterdam, and yet he is infatuated with U.S. Route 66, so much so that he had a rendering of the iconic Painted Desert Trading Post boldly tattooed on his upper arm.

"I have traveled all over the world, and the U.S. is my favorite," says Dries. "The people are (almost always) friendly, the countryside is great and travel is easy. The first time I rode all of Route 66 by motorcycle was the best vacation I've had in my life."

Dries and his wife, Marion, traveled Route 66 last year and plan to return this year. They were surprised when they started the route in Chicago and saw a sign that declared Chicago the "End of the Road." The couple headed west, with Dries straddling a brand-new (rented) Electra motorcycle, his wife in a "ZZ-Top." In Springfield, they met up with friends to tour the Dana-Thomas House, reminiscent of California's Winchester House, and attended a local bike show.

Their travels took them to Route 66 sites such as a replica of Stonehenge, Becky's Barn, Fast Freddies, the world's largest rocking chair and a ride along the Mississippi River. "On the bridge between Galena and Baxter Springs, we met Dean Walker, a man who can rotate his legs so his feet point backward. In Oklahoma, we saw empty buildings, often derelict and long since abandoned," Dries recalls.

They stopped to see the world's largest totem pole, "not exactly the nicest, but it sure is big!" They loved a diner in St. James called Diana's, and they stayed at the Big Texan in Amarillo, "which I would recommend to anybody." They visited the Cadillac Ranch, the Bug

Ranch (as in VWs) and a graveyard for combine harvesters. "Boy, what Americans come up with when they are bored," he said.

Dries and Marion veered off Route 66, taking Route 104 "since Route 66 is under heavy construction." Through the mountains toward Las Vegas, New Mexico, they ran into freezing weather with low visibility, but "by the time the sun came out, we were in a very nice adobe motel."

They traveled through the Painted Desert, stopped at the Wig Wam hotel in Holbrook, stood on the corner in Winslow, Arizona, and met up with Jim Hinckley of the Kingman Route 66 Association. They continued on to Oatman (the burro-friendly town outside Laughlin) and on to Barstow, where "we found the bottle forest which displays tree-like structures made of metal and bottles."

He explains Los Angeles as "a place you encounter a traffic light on almost every block, programmed to turn red when you get in the vicinity," and finally, after 2,284 miles, they reached Santa Monica, the end of the route, "or is it the beginning?"

"Route 66 is so enjoyable," he says. "It takes you through varied landscapes, from the green lands of Missouri to the mountains of New Mexico and the desert of Arizona. Along the way, you get to encounter doses of true Americana from a time when life seemed much simpler."

Time Travel: The Sagebrush Annie Stretch

From the Do-Drop Inn to Sagebrush Annie's Sagebrush Inn, from the former site of the burlesque museum to the town of Oro Grande, there lies a remote stretch of Old Route 66 between Barstow and Victorville that remains today much as it was in the late 1920s. Here you can drive the highway and feel yourself transported back in time.

Modern maps reveal little more in the area than vacant land and desert air, yet this stretch of Route 66 embraces a colorful history framed by prohibition, the Great Depression and World War II. Buried in the sand and sagebrush are relics of days gone by. Adding to the intrigue is the saga of Sagebrush Annie, owner of the Sagebrush Inn.

The town of Helendale began as a Santa Fe siding and was named for the daughter of that railroad's general manager. In the 1950s, the town dwindled to fewer than 250 residents, but before it withered away

The Polly gas parrot sign remains on the Sagebrush Annie stretch of Route 66. He seems to be smirking, while passersby envy the posted price of gas: "REG. 18.9; ETHYL: 21.9."

completely, the resort of Silver Lakes was built and the population soared. To the chagrin of the residents, it was the home of the Exotic Dancer Museum, which has since moved to Las Vegas.

Along the Mother Road, Polly the Parrot, the mascot for the Polly brand of gasoline, appears to laugh at those of us who pull over to snap a photo of the sign, which boasts the price of gas: "REG. 18.9; ETHYL: 21.9."

Between Helendale and Oro Grande, the colorful tales emanate. During the peak years of Route 66 (1926 to the mid-1940s), Sagebrush Annie was said to be a successful businesswoman, taking advantage of the steady stream of Route 66 travelers headed to Los Angeles and Hollywood. Her establishment, the Sagebrush Inn, was rumored to boast many uses, such as a café, a nightclub, a service station, a residence and even more questionable enterprises. The stone columns and walls still stand at Annie's abode. The weathered wood sign and gas pumps have long since disappeared. Only the stone foundation of Sagebrush Annie's remains, and it is now a private residence.

For an in-depth account of the historical background of the area, purchase a copy of *The Story of Sagebrush Annie and the Sagebrush Route* by Richard D. Thompson at the Victorville Route 66 Museum or the

Sagebrush Annie's infamous abode remains today as a private residence. However, the weathered wooden sign and gas pumps have long since disappeared.

California Route 66 Museum in Barstow. In addition, both museums offer a detailed map of the thirty-five-mile stretch showing the sites of interest.

Heading west, a stop at the Bottle Tree Ranch is a tourist must. Before reaching Oro Grande, you will pass the Iron Hog Saloon, a former Case Farm Equipment dealership that flourished in the 1930s and '40s. A few miles to the west are the Riverside Cement Company and underpass. Look for the steel-truss bridge, built in 1930, that spans the Mojave River.

The town of Oro Grande was built on hopes that gold would sustain it, but time would prove that the oro wasn't so grand, and the town faded. A worthwhile stop at the site is the Route 66 Antique Station, which offers scads of Route 66 items.

DAN HYKE: PEDALING ALONG ROUTE 66

Dealing with the pain of his father's death, Dan Hyke, then age twenty-nine, took to the road, determined to conquer a monumental feat. He pedaled his bicycle to the beach, dipped the rear tire into the Pacific

Ocean and then headed east. Sixty days later, he dipped his front tire into the Atlantic Ocean at Virginia Beach. What happened in between was a turning point in his life. The year was 1982, and Dan set off to follow Route 66 and then the Bikecentennial route through Colorado, Kansas, Missouri, Kentucky and Virginia. The latter route was mapped in 1976 when four thousand bicyclists pedaled across the nation. Dan carried a journal in which he wrote daily, documenting his thoughts, money spent each day, addresses of people he met along the way and daily mileage. His average daily expenditure was $19.59. Dan traveled with a friend through the Mojave Desert, visiting old Mother Road towns such as Essex, Amboy, Goffs and Needles. In Arizona, they rode through Kingman and Oatman. At the Grand Canyon, the pair decided to part because Dan wanted to travel at a slower pace.

"I remember the Navajo children selling turquoise and silver jewelry," Dan says. He traveled on the Old Route 66 and nearby small roads accompanied by "an original Walkman." Carrying a small tent, Dan camped along the way, and "in those days you could get all-you-can-eat

Dan Hyke dipped his rear bike tire into the Pacific Ocean before heading east on Route 66. After pedaling through Chicago, he continued to the coast and there, in a private act of ceremony, dipped his front wheel into the Atlantic Ocean. *Courtesy of Dan Hyke.*

salad bar at the Pizza Hut for two dollars." He would occasionally stay in a motel when he felt the need for a hot shower and a soft bed.

Traveling 3,560 miles, Dan experienced only one flat tire on his ten-speed Nishiki. Daily he covered from 50 to 60 miles, although one day he pedaled 121 miles. He recalls riding through the wheat fields of Kansas on a moonless night when he couldn't even see the road in front of him. "The fireflies were flickering all around me," he recalls. In Kansas, he camped in the city parks, which was allowed at the time.

Wind was Dan's worst enemy. "It wasn't like the winds here, which come and go," he recalls. "Strong winds would blow for days, making progress very difficult." He was also buffeted from gusts created by large speeding trucks and would have to pull off the road if he spied them in his rearview mirror. He used his air pump to ward off pursuing dogs.

By the time he finally reached Virginia Beach, his life had changed forever. "I learned several important lessons on that trip," lessons that he teaches his students. "Never give up. Be persistent in following your dreams. Overcome your personal fears. Face the challenges before you."

Today, Dan is the head of the science department at Alhambra High School, where he teaches environmental science. He says that pedaling on Route 66 and beyond changed his life for the better. He keeps his journal close at hand as a reminder of that fateful trip, and he enjoys the enthusiasm of his students when he shows them a slide show of the journey.

Route 66 travelers have trekked the highway in many ways. They have driven cars, walked, ran, motorcycled, bicycled, jogged and skated. But Dan is satisfied with his mode of transportation, which allowed him to see America at a slow pace, take advantage of a largely abandoned Route 66 and meet other cyclists along the way.

Victorville: Past and Present

Emerging from the Sagebrush Annie portion of Route 66, it is a shock to cross the Mojave River on the steel-truss bridge into the thriving town of Victorville. Before railroads, this crossing of the Mojave River was called "Mormon Crossing." Before rail, the site that became Victorville operated as a "station," welcoming visitors for a fee.

Named after the desert area construction supervisor, Jacob Nash Victor, the area was called Victor and later changed to Victorville. When Route 66 was established, it was the result of linking many roads together, resulting in one continuous highway running from Chicago to Los Angeles and beyond. The stretch through Victorville was the National Trails Highway, which, when connected to the other roads to form Route 66, brought with it a stream of westbound motorists.

To meet the demand of these travelers, garages, cafés, motels and gas stations blossomed. Driving through town today, one can see evidence of the hospitality that this town offered visitors. The New Corral Hotel stands proudly as a Route 66 classic that boasts a Wild West that embraced Victorville in the past. Today, its sign looms over the road as a nostalgic reminder of another day.

Filled with hard-core volunteers mostly knowledgeable in Route 66 history is the staff at the California Route 66 Museum located in Old Town Victorville on D Street between Fifth and Sixth Streets. Books, maps and memorabilia abound, and in-depth exhibits will keep you busy for hours. Close to home is the section featuring artifacts from the Trails Restaurant, the Route 66 icon that attracted patrons from near and far to dine in the San Gabriel Valley town of Duarte. The museum has on display the wagon wheel chandelier, the original stick sign, a menu and one of the Tiffany lamps that adorned the restaurant since its opening in 1952. Sadly, it was demolished in 2001.

On the town's eastern outskirts is Emma Jean's truck stop, which was once boasted as home of the Brian Burger but today advertises the Holland Burger. Built in 1947 by Bob and Emma Jean Holland, this café has been the scene of several movies and television shows, including *Kill Bill 2* and shows on the Food Network. The generous portions of food made from scratch attract locals, as well as today's Route 66 travelers looking for a blast from the past.

As fast as the National Trails Highway morphed into Route 66, Highway 15 plunged a knife into the heart of the Mother Road when it beckoned motorists to a smoother, faster and newer highway. Today, most motorists do not stop in Victorville as they head for the gateway to Los Angeles. Just as motorists of the past yearned for bigger and better, more and more of today's travelers are abandoning the need for speed and embracing a slower pace to enjoy the sights of America along its Main Street.

VERCILLO: HISTORY IN THE MAKING

Mike Vercillo, a resident of Arcadia since 1967, fondly remembers the trip his family took in 1955 on Route 66 from Chicago to California. "As a young lad of twelve, my greatest anticipation was to see American Indians out west. I immediately fell in love with their baskets, silver jewelry and colorful blankets," he says. Since those days, he has researched Indian crafted blankets and found himself enlightened as to the meaning behind their colors, designs and weaves, "all of which tell a purposeful story."

En route to his grandparents' sixty-five-acre grape ranch in Fontana, "we rode in an older Ford [late '20s], and my uncle drove a brand-new 1955 bright yellow Pontiac," recalls Mike. He remembers the canvas water bag hanging off the hood ornament, "which my father said we might need when we crossed the desert." It was traditional for Route 66 travelers to hang a water bag from the car. In a way, it was a status symbol, but it could also be a lifesaver in the searing heat of the California desert. The family stayed in small motor lodges along the way. He recalls that although some were quite festive with their theme-laden architecture, "we found a few of them to be roach-infested. Aunt Millie, normally a quiet and diminutive person, turned into a modern-day gladiator, who, with rolled-up newspaper in hand, attacked those insects with a vengeance. I never quite viewed her in the same way again."

Eating three meals a day along the road, Mike says that his favorite was lunch, which never varied from a hamburger, French fries and a chocolate shake. "We didn't worry about a heart attack or cholesterol numbers in those days."

Mike and his wife were both raised in Chicago. When Mike's older sister came to California to see him, she traveled Route 66, and "it was great to hear her recount her travels across the Old Route."

Like many who recall travels on the Mother Road, Mike's memories have become philosophical. "When one experiences history in the making, it is not normally viewed as such until years later. With decades now behind me, I have fondly looked back to that trip and a few trips before that time, which have enriched my life and appreciation of this great country and its Mother Road."

Planning on retirement in the next few years, Mike and his wife are collecting books and articles to guide them on a future trip to retrace as much of Route 66 as they can. He feels that he will then be able to write about his memories on the Mother Road from the view of both a child and an adult.

"So much has been told about Route 66 by those who have traveled its colorful miles, as well as by those who have retold the stories of others, that little more can be said other than to relate the memories of those still living, who have benefited by its encounter," says Mike.

The Cajon Pass: A Trail of Strange Bedfellows

Travel through the Cajon Pass has always been treacherous. Plagued with rocky paths, steep grades and nearly impassable canyons, the corridor has been negotiated with great difficulty by Indians, Spanish explorers, missionaries, trappers, pioneers and adventurers. Even modern-day motorists are intimidated when this gateway from the high desert to the lowlands is the subject of fog, snow, ice, floods or wildfires.

With the San Gabriel Mountains looming to the west and the San Bernardino Mountains rising to the east, this road has a colorful history, from its beginnings as the Old Spanish Trail to the Mormon Crossing, Route 66 and Interstate 15. Those who have left their mark on the area's history are strange bedfellows and include Jedediah Smith, Kit Carson, John C. Frémont, Peg-Leg Smith, Hilda Fish and Sammy Davis Jr. Add into the mix horses, mules and camels.

Pioneers traveling from Salt Lake to Los Angeles utilized the pass under the protection of the Mormon Battalion. Later, stagecoaches and the U.S. Mail Service arrived, followed by merchants moving their goods west. At one time, the corridor was a toll road. In 1855, traffic had increased to the point that funds were expended to improve the wagon road, making for easier travel.

The first paved road was built in 1920, and Route 66 was dedicated in 1926. Portions of the road were washed out in the catastrophic flood of 1938. Although motorists today must drive on I-15, there are a few sections of Old Route 66 still in use. On the east side of Cajon Junction, you can turn south onto the frontage road, which dead-ends at the Mormon Trail Marker.

Or take the Cleghorn Road exit and drive a section of 66 along Cajon Creek, where you can cross some historic bridges. There is also a section along Swarthout Canyon Road, which was the site of an old migrant workers' camp during the Depression.

Step back into time and relive the heyday of Route 66, when you visit the Summit Inn, located at the crest of the pass at the Oak Street exit. Next door to this iconic eatery is a vintage building, once a Texaco station. The inn is typical of Mother Road eateries and features lumpy seats, coin-operated fortunetelling machines, a gift shop and menu items such as ostrich omelets and buffalo steaks.

Hilda Fish was the anchor waitress for thirty-eight years. Her beehive hairstyle and friendly personality welcomed such patrons as Elvis Presley, Pierce Brosnan and Pearl Bailey. Fish retired in 2002 and is now deceased.

Leaving the pass, slow down and reflect a moment on the fate of one of Hollywood's favorite entertainers, Sammy Davis Jr. In 1952, returning to Los Angeles from a gig in Las Vegas, he was involved in a car accident at a fork on Route 66 at Cajon Boulevard and Kendall Drive. The crash, which nearly left him dead, resulted in the loss of his left eye. He wore a patch for a while and then a glass eye. He continued entertaining until his death in 1990.

Part IV
San Bernardino to Azusa

San Bernardino: Champion of the Mother Road

There are probably few Route 66 towns between Santa Monica and Chicago that embrace the heritage of the Mother Road more than San Bernardino. For four days every September, the town's Route 66 Rendezvous attracts more than 250,000 visitors and more than two thousand classic cars.

Traveling west through the Cajon Pass, Route 66 intermittently merges with I-15, leaving the clear skies of the high desert behind and emerging into the hazy, sprawling city of San Bernardino. Along the route now marked as Mount Vernon Avenue, scores of dilapidated remnants of once thriving garages, cafés and motels remain. A few mom and pop businesses continue to serve the public, such as the Mitla Café, established in 1937.

Sure to awaken memories of the past is the Original McDonald's Site Museum at 1398 North E Street on the business loop of Route 66. Thousands of artifacts from the humble beginnings of this mega chain are on display. This is the original site of McDonald's, owned by the McDonald brothers. It opened as the Airdrome in 1940 and was converted to the first McDonald's in 1948. The story goes, "It was here that Ray Kroc tried to sell Dick and Mac McDonald a MixMaster [a milkshake machine] in 1954 and ended up buying their name."

Before this, the McDonald brothers opened their first restaurant (the Airdrome) in 1937 at a private airport located in Monrovia.

There the brothers sold hot dogs, orange juice, coffee and tea. In 1940, they moved the Airdrome to San Bernardino, naming it the McDonald's Barbeque Restaurant. Several years later, to capitalize on the popularity of their hamburgers and fries, they switched to McDonald's Hamburgers, and this led to the opening of McDonald's in Phoenix, Arizona; North Hollywood; and Downey. The Downey McDonald's remains open for business, the oldest-surviving McDonald's in the world.

Here Route 66 history merges. The McDonald's Museum was established by a champion of Route 66 survival, Albert Okura, owner of Juan Pollo. Okura also bought the town of Amboy along Route 66 in the Mojave Desert and is restoring that iconic town. The McDonald's Museum is open daily, and admission is free.

The growth of San Bernardino was greatly spurred by the arrival of the railroad in the 1880s, which propelled it into becoming an important trade center. San Bernardino changed from a sleepy town to an enterprising city. In 1883, the Southern Pacific arrived in Colton, and in 1885, the Santa Fe completed its line through the Cajon Pass into the city itself. Today's visitors are reminded of this town's railroad history when they see the imposing smokestack, which still looms over the area. It was part of a roundhouse that has been destroyed.

THE OUTRAGEOUS BUNION DERBY

Perhaps one of the most incredible events in the history of Route 66 is C.C. Pyle's Amazing Foot Race, better known as the Bunion Derby. This coast-to-coast run across America took place in 1928 as a publicity stunt, attracting participants with a $25,000 prize to the winner.

Leslie Clemmer, a resident of West Covina since 1960, was nine years old when his elementary school class in Willow, Oklahoma, was herded onto a school bus for a field trip to the nearby Route 66 town of Sayre. "It was around noon when the runners sprinted by," he recalls.

His young mind entertained many thoughts about the runners, such as what kind of shoes they wore and how many petered out. To this day, he remembers that the runners were in very good physical condition, although many dropped out because of injuries or pure exhaustion.

Conceived as a marketing ploy, runners were enticed into participating in the Bunion Derby, a foot race from Los Angeles to the Atlantic, by a first-place prize of $25,000. The contest winner was Andrew Payne, part Cherokee Indian from Foyil, Oklahoma.

Although 500,000 spectators lined a stretch of Route 66 in Los Angeles to see the runners off, public interest waned as the race headed east. Pyle's plan to earn a fortune on the event ended in disappointment. He had hoped that financial gain would result from entrance fees, the sale of programs and endorsements from advertisers of foot cream, suntan lotion and, perhaps, bunion pads.

The race covered 3,400 miles, approximately 2,400 of which were on Route 66. Over half of the runners had dropped out by the third day. Torrential rains and searing heat took their toll.

In the end, twenty-year-old Andrew Hartley Payne, part Cherokee Indian, was the winner, averaging six miles per hour. His closest competitor, a Brit named Peter Gavuzzi, dropped out in Ohio. Born and raised in Foyil, Oklahoma, Payne was greeted by the mayor and crowds of well-wishers when he reached his home state. The race did not stop in Chicago but continued on to New York. Crossing the finish line hours ahead of the other participants, Payne had run for a total of 573 hours, 4 minutes and 34 seconds.

Clemmer, now ninety-three, never forgot the thrill of watching the runners. Fifteen years ago, he traveled in his RV to the Oklahoma town of Tahlequah, and there he visited the Cherokee Heritage Center to see a statue of Payne. Another statue of Payne stands in his hometown of Foyil, and every year an Andrew Payne Bunion Run marathon is held in Oklahoma City. In 1998, a committee made up of runners voted Payne among the first on the Oklahoma Long Distance Running Wall of Fame in Tulsa.

"Payne's $25,000 prize was a great deal of money in those days," says Clemmer. "Gas in California at that time was nine cents a gallon." It is said that Payne used the money to pay off the mortgage on his parents' farm. "I am amazed that with all of the articles I have read on Highway 66, I have never read about the foot race that took place on that highway," says Clemmer. The story is now out! In 2007, a book by Geoff Williams was released with the title *C.C. Pyle's Amazing Foot Race*. This is the first in-depth book about the race.

This great foot race is yet another tale of how the highway has transcended beyond mere asphalt. It has encouraged entrepreneurs to come up with the most imaginative of ideas, and it has beckoned dreamers to reach for their goals.

RIALTO AND FONTANA AND WIGWAMS

There is little change of scenery along Route 66 when you leave San Bernardino and head into the towns of Rialto and Fontana. Expect a few surprises and some nostalgic gems, but there is no underlying theme, and unkempt business buildings are often flanked by vacant lots with thriving weeds. Both towns, however, reap the scenic advantage of their backdrop: the stunning San Bernardino Mountains.

In Rialto, there are hints of a town that once enjoyed an abundance of successes. Numerous small motels line the route, a few with covered parking garages alongside the rooms. Diners, cafés, gas stations and auto repair shops abound. And yes, there are the occasional iconic surprises

One of the road's most famous oddities is the Wigwam Motel in Rialto, which serves overnighters today as it did in the past.

that are testaments to the town's attempt to assist travelers and make a buck to boot. The time from the 1920s to the 1960s was busy for Rialto.

Although there is some controversy as to whether the Wigwam Motel is located in San Bernardino or Rialto, let's assume it is on the west side of the border. It exists today as a reminder of the creative minds that sought to attract travelers during the road's major days. The teepees are well kept, and who would not want to say that they, at least once, slept in a teepee?

The city of Rialto was established in 1887 by the Semi-Tropic Land and Water Company, which brought water from Lytle Creek to surrounding cities. The Hotel del Rialto was constructed that year. It burned down in 1907. The city was once known for its lemon groves, which produced crops so abundant that they required seven local packinghouses.

Leaving Rialto, the merge into Fontana is subtle. The two towns share a common history. Before 1905, Fontana was named Rosena. Its current name was adopted in 1905 when the Fontana Development Company purchased the land and obtained water rights. The town was incorporated in 1952 after it had developed into one of the largest chicken- and pig-raising areas in the West. It has since become an industrial and residential community.

In the world of Route 66 buffs, the main icons in Fontana are Bono's Restaurant and Deli, which opened for business in 1936, and the nearby juice stand. Shaped like a large orange, that stand is a reminder of the days when the sweet and tangy nectar was served to thirsty motorists traveling through a valley known for its excellent citrus ranches. Over the years, many juice stands along the Mother Road morphed into restaurants. The surviving juice stand is no longer in service but today attracts photographers from near and far.

By the time eastern travelers reached Rialto and Fontana, they were near the end of their journey. If they had headed west believing the rumors of a multitude of jobs available in Los Angeles, many families would be sadly disappointed.

CUCAMONGA, FORMERLY TIMBUKTU

There was a time when Cucamonga was synonymous with "the boondocks" or "Timbuktu." Cucamonga was also repeatedly the butt of jokes on television and radio. However, Cucamonga has now had the last laugh. With the dynamic eight-thousand-foot Cucamonga peak of the San Gabriel Mountains as a backdrop, that town has added "Rancho" to its name and enjoys the convenience of two major freeways, a booming population, numerous parks, upscale malls and shopping centers and a state-of-the-art community theater. And to keep in touch with its history, RC enthusiastically celebrates Route 66, which stretches between its borders.

In 1977, the communities of Alta Loma, Cucamonga and Etiwanda voted to incorporate as a single city to be known as Rancho Cucamonga, a vote that passed despite initial resistance in Alta Loma. By 1990, Rancho Cucamonga's population had reached 115,000, and today more than 180,000 residents call it home.

Rancho Cucamonga is a historical location where California's most famous trails and roads converge: the Mojave Trail, the Spanish Trail, the El Camino Real, the Santa Fe Trail, the Butterfield Stagecoach Route and U.S. Highway Route 66. Cucamonga is a Shoshone word that has been translated into two seemingly opposite meanings: "a sandy place" and "land of many waters."

The Sycamore Inn in Rancho Cucamonga was established in 1848 and served as a Butterfield Stage stop. It serves patrons today in the same friendly manner as in the past.

The town recently lost a historical icon when its eighty-one-year-old Pacific Electric Railway bridge, which spanned the Mother Road, was dismantled to be replaced by a more modern one as part of a street-widening project. In the name of history, a portion of the old bridge will be on display at a nearby park on the north side of Route 66.

Along the route, stone pillars display the Route 66 shield, and many local businesses proudly exhibit the iconic highway marker. Two famed Route 66 restaurants remain open today, offering patrons an opportunity to enjoy an ambience reminiscent of the route's heyday. The Sycamore Inn, originally a stagecoach stop, dates back to 1848 and hold memories for many old-timers. Charles Stein was born in Chicago and came west on Route 66 with his family in 1929. He was a resident of Arcadia for thirty-five years and presently resides in Bradbury.

"I've traveled Route 66 back and forth from Arcadia to Chicago many times over the years," says Stein. He fondly recalls the Sycamore Inn in Rancho Cucamonga during the era when Route 66 was the main highway. Established in 1848, it was a Butterfield Stage stop. Stein recalls the inn's charming and rustic ambience, which has greeted travelers for generations and continues to do so today.

The Magic Lamp Restaurant in Rancho Cucamonga was opened in 1957 and remains open today.

Stein also has fond memories of riding on the Pacific Electric Red Cars from Arcadia to Santa Monica. "The Red Car tracks followed Route 66 during those days," he recalls.

The Magic Lamp Inn opened in 1957. A restored one-hundred-year-old farmhouse, now the Route 66 Memories gift shop, is located there and offers a variety of Route 66 memorabilia and information.

Wineries are a part of RC's history, and although most vineyards have disappeared, their legacies remain. The Thomas Winery is designated as a historic California landmark as the oldest commercial winery in the state and the second-oldest in the nation. Today, the Wine Tailor operates in the old Thomas Winery building. The Virginia Dare Winery was located on Route 66 and was the site where the old 1960s TV show *Combat* was filmed. The building now serves as a shopping center.

As a tribute to its history, the city launched a public arts mural program for the Route 66 corridor and supports the project with financial assistance.

Transformed from a land of vineyards and wide-open spaces, the flourishing town of Rancho Cucamonga basks in its successes but also honors its past and the highway that brought motorists west.

A Swede, a Trek and a Journal

Axel Sterner traveled from his home in Sweden in 1912 to begin a new life in New York, a trip that was no doubt eventful. Later, in 1927, Axel and his wife, Beda, undertook another monumental journey. They traveled from New York to Los Angeles by car, partially along the newly commissioned Route 66.

Fortunately, for the sake of history, Axel spent time each evening of the journey entering the day's events in his journal. His poignant account of the trek might have been lost to the world were it not for his grandniece by marriage, Ethel Whitson, who recognized its historic value and coveted the writings among her favorite possessions. A resident of Whittier for fifty years, Ethel has lived in Bradbury for the last decade. She had hoped that someday this personal account of travel before modern cars and amenities would be published for others to enjoy. She carefully typed the contents of the journal, "misspellings and all, in his Swedish/American interpretation." His writings reflect the language and spelling as written.

Axel and Beda traveled in one car, followed by his niece and cousin in another. After a day of travel, the party would set up camp, and Axel would chronicle the day's events in his journal. In Missouri, he wrote:

> *Left campground at 6:50 a.m. Fine weather all day but hot. The lady's has been feeling pretty fidgety all day. Had trouble getting out of Joilet. Started back for Chicago at first but did not go far before seeing our mistake…* [That day he recorded 213 miles including a detour.]
>
> *Over the McKinley Bridge they charged us 50 cents to cross the Mississippi River…then thru St. Louis and out thru Natural Bridge Road over Missouri River where they soaked us another 50 cents to cross.*
>
> [Road hazards were plenty.] *Today was the first day we have had the real test of the durt roads and we will have plenty for some time to come. I had my first flat tire to day and was skidding round the road like a drunken man…and that cost me 75 cents.* [That night, they stopped for] *our Fourth of July dinner which was chicken…all for 75 cents what would have cost us at least $1.25 in New York.*

He wrote about the severe weather, which ranged from frost to searing heat, and mechanical trouble was never far away. They were plagued with dust, mosquitoes and campgrounds with showers so dirty that the women refused to enter. In Chicago, he wrote:

> *Laying up today to see Chicago and for me to get my rear end raised up as I was hitting the axle housing at every little hole as hit on the road so I had an extra leaf put in the rear spring and also brackets on truck rack, with cost me $15.00.*

There were days the party lodged in cabins, which ran about one dollar a night for the four of them, a treat after a day of 213 miles of travel. Throughout the journal, he recorded meal prices, with lunch running about thirty cents per person, dinner seventy-five cents. He talked of getting his car washed at the "auto laundry" and of one harrowing experience when he was "trying to avoid a rut and the frontwheel got a little too close to the edge of the road so the earth gave away—no damage done."

His journal has the look of a family heirloom, stitched together on the left with needle and thread to make a book. It is titled "From New York City to San Diego, Calif. Via. Auto By Axel J. Sterner, 1927. Started June 20th, 1927. Arrived July 20th 1927."

Ethel believes that her "Uncle Axel" was born in the 1880s and died in about 1949. She continues to research the family history.

Note: After this story appeared in the Highlander *newspaper, a reader obtained a copy of Uncle Axel's birth certificate and sent it to Ethel. Also, she was contacted by the Autry Museum, and arrangements were made for this historical journal to be stored in the museum's repository, where it will remain as a permanent record.*

SAVING ICONS IN UPLAND AND CLAREMONT

The Route 66 community of Upland is commonly characterized as a small rural town. Located in western San Bernardino County, it sits in the shadow of Mount Baldy and retains much of the charm for which it was deemed desirable in its early days. Adobe- and ranch-style homes remain in contrast to modern housing developments. This town actively celebrates its Route 66 heritage, saving many of the road's icons that once punctuated its efforts to serve travelers of the past.

Originally promoted as Magnolia Villa, the town became known as North Ontario in 1887. It became a city in 1902 and, to avoid annexation to Ontario, changed its name to Upland, in reference to its higher elevation.

In an effort to modernize strip malls and shopping squares, Upland has revitalized its section of Route 66 and in the mix has retained several icons. Of note is the Buffalo Inn, which dates back to 1929. This establishment enjoys more raves about the frontier-saloon atmosphere than the food, with one stating, "The Buffalo Inn, saved from extinction 18 years ago by owner Forest Rinard, is perhaps the most inviting, atmospheric, kick-back comfortable experience this side of Claremont."

Upland is anchored by the famed Madonna of the Trail statue, a memorial to pioneer women that sits on the corner of Route 66 and Euclid. On a recent Route 66 trip, I was surprised to find a mirror image of the statue in downtown Albuquerque. I came to find out that there are twelve of these statues throughout the country. In Upland, the statue officially marks the end of the National Trails Highway, the precursor to Route 66.

Just west of Upland is the campus-rich town of Claremont, located on the Los Angeles County line. Here, Route 66 has been characterized as "one of the most beautiful original sections of the existing route." Today, as in the route's heyday, it offers a shady drive under a towering canopy of eucalyptus in contrast to the hot, dusty desert towns that greeted motorists traveling west. It is perhaps this quiet beauty that encouraged motorists migrating from points east to stop and consider planting their roots in Claremont.

Founded in 1878 by the Pacific Land and Improvement Company, water was reportedly hauled into the fledgling town to serve to travelers. Today, the town's population is known to be creative and educated, anchored by several college campuses and commonly referred to as the cultural arts center of the Pomona Valley. More humorously, it is referred to as "the city of trees and PhDs."

Celebrating its stretch of America's Highway, historic Route 66 signs are posted along the corridor, and businesses proudly display the shield, which is also stenciled onto the road. Such icons as family-owned and family-operated Wolfe's Market, in business since 1917, remain. This establishment was relocated to its present spot, on the south side of Route 66, in 1935.

Along the route, today's visitors make a point to stop at the town's landmark, the Claremont Inn and Old Schoolhouse complex, which serves as a shopping center and is anchored by the Candlelight Pavilion.

Wolfe's Market in Upland has remained in business since 1917. It was relocated to its present spot in 1935.

The Schoolhouse was originally Claremont High School, built in 1911 and brought up to earthquake standards in 1931, the year Route 66 was officially opened in that town. The popular Candlelight Pavilion is housed in what was the school's gymnasium.

DUST BOWL: THE WORST OF HARD TIMES

Television delivered the devastation and horror of Katrina's assault on New Orleans into our homes, compelling the world to share the pain of those in its wake. In 1930, thousands of victims of another major disaster struggled to stay alive, not for a week or a month, but for nearly a decade. If they had the resources to escape, they were often humiliated, rejected and turned away. Much of the world turned a blind eye.

Route 66 was commissioned in 1926, and in 1930 America's Highway was still in ragtag condition in many places. With the mass production of automobiles and roadside amenities blossoming along the route, motorists headed west to seek better opportunities or merely to visit the wonders of the country. But there were those who took to the road to escape what came to be termed "the great Dust Bowl," which forced families to abandon their homesteads.

As John Steinbeck wrote in his historic novel *The Grapes of Wrath*, "Route 66 was the path of people in flight, refugees from dust and shrinking land." In Oklahoma, Texas, Kansas and the surrounding areas, the 1930s was the decade from hell.

Attributed to a prolonged and severe drought, coupled with the continuous devastation of the prairie grasslands due to overplowing, horrific dust storms choked the earth with dry, unanchored soil that was carried by raging winds and wreaked havoc on humans, animals and farm equipment. The public started to take notice when a two-hundred-mile-wide "roller" crossed into Kansas and then caused the temperature in Denver to drop twenty degrees as the city was plunged into darkness. Dodge City went black as the two-thousand-foot-high "duster" was clocked at sixty-five miles per hour; barbed wire fences glowed with electricity.

For those who remained in the affected area, life was a battle. Children and animals died of "dust pneumonia." No crops could grow. Livestock, bellies filled with dirt, starved to death. Families, strangled by the dust, begged for help, but sympathy was in short supply. Some believed that they were living the prophecy expounded by Sitting Bull, who predicted that the land would get its revenge on the whites who had forced the Indians off the grasslands.

In May 1933, far-off rain clouds raced across the sky, and as the drops picked up dust, mud globs smashed rooftops, dented car hoods and caused livestock to cry in agony. Stores were pulverized into piles of sticks. A year later, another monumental set of whirlwinds caught the world's attention. In the Dakotas and eastern Montana, a mass of dust-filled clouds blew east, picking up strength as it approached population centers. Hitting Illinois and Ohio, pilots described the scene as "a solid block of airborne dirt." Planes were forced to fly above fifteen thousand feet to escape the dust storm, which dumped an estimated six thousand tons of dirt; by morning, dust fell like snow over Boston, Scranton and New York. Finally, the world took notice.

While Route 66 offered a road to escape, few had the means to do so. The road beckoned with false promises. Families with the ability to flee the land of dusters were met with disdain when reaching the "promise land of the West." They faced prejudice and poverty but, happily, no dust.

The Worst Hard Times (The Untold Story of Those Who Survived the Great American Dust Bowl) by Timothy Egan was described as "a classic disaster tale" by the *New York Times*. It tells the story of the plight of individual families who lost everything.

Today, there is little evidence that a disaster occurred. All along Route 66 in Texas, Oklahoma, Kansas and Missouri, cornfields and other crops form a sea of lush green. Modern planting techniques guard against a recurrence of a seemingly forgotten disaster, and once more the earth appears to be at peace (in that regard).

LA VERNE, SAN DIMAS: ONCE THE WILD WEST

For westbound Route 66 travelers headed for "the good life in Southern California," reaching the San Gabriel Valley city of La Verne, some thirty-five miles east of Los Angeles, must have been a milestone. When the kids asked, "Are we there yet?" the answer could now in truth be, "Yes."

Founded in 1887 and incorporated in 1906, the town was originally called Lordsburg after Isaac Wilson Lord, who made a fortune selling his real estate holdings when the Santa Fe Railway extended its line to the area. In 1916, the name was changed to La Verne after a promoter of nearby La Verne Heights.

With the commissioning of Route 66, which ribboned through the citrus ranches of La Verne, garages, restaurants and motor courts sprung up, as they did in many towns along the route. Today, there are remnants of those entities as a reminder of the glory days of the Mother Road, such as the La Paloma Restaurant located in La Verne. Once called Wilson's Restaurant, it has been serving travelers since 1966.

Today, foothill motorists passing under the I-210 Freeway find themselves on the route in the wannabe Wild West town of San Dimas, originally known as Mud Springs. In addition to treasuring its Route 66 legacy, this town has revived its history, evident in the Old

West architecture displayed in the downtown area, including wooden sidewalks and false wood storefronts.

A favorite steakhouse on America's Highway is located in San Dimas. Pinnacle Peak is a landmark of the Wild West kind, anchored by a wagon train. It sits on the site of an old Wells Fargo stage stop and has been serving travelers for more than four decades. And gentlemen, don't wear a tie to this establishment or it will be clipped and hung on the wall.

Just west of San Dimas is a town that has proved to be earnestly dedicated to preserving its Route 66 history. The city of Glendora, in a controversial move, undertook the monumental step of readopting the street name of Route 66 and subbing it formally, retiring the street signs for Alosta Avenue. This trend is often bucked by businesses and residents because of the paperwork and cost inherent in such a name change, but Glendora did the deed, adding credibility to its Route 66 highway markers.

Established in 1887 when the railroad arrived, Glendora blossomed when its portion of Route 66 was officially dedicated. While old motor courts, cafés and garages have largely disappeared from the scene, some survived as viable businesses. Of the many Mother Road establishments celebrated on the route, the Golden Spur Restaurant, 1223 East Route 66, remains a favorite, still in business after eighty years. No longer is it a hamburger stand on a dirt road where classic cars and horses once graced its quarters. Today, patrons enjoy a little peek into the ambience enjoyed during quieter days gone by.

The Everlasting Marketing Ploy

There is a slice of Americana along Route 66 that has historically captivated the hearts and minds of travelers. Even today, though the product has disappeared and the signs removed, the marketing ploy of posting Burma-Shave rhymes along highways has remained a favorite memory. Burma-Shave signs once helped keep drivers alert and kids entertained while promoting a brand of brushless shaving cream sold from 1925 to 1966.

Such innovation! Typically a row of signs, usually six in number, was erected along the roadside to be read sequentially by motorists. Each of the first five would contain a line of the rhyme, and the sixth would simply say, "Burma-Shave." Most advertising is considered annoying, but there are a few creative slogans that seem to catch on and become embedded in the brain.

Burma-Shave signs could be seen along the nation's highways from 1925 to 1966. When the new interstates came into play, driving speeds made reading the signs difficult. Those remaining today are usually sponsored by historical entities such as museums.

Burma-Shave signs appeared along highways throughout most of the forty-eight states starting in 1925. At the height of their popularity, they numbered more than seven thousand signs, and motorists were constantly on the lookout, seeking to spot a series and read the rhyme out loud.

The Burma-Vita Company was founded by Clinton Odell and his sons. Hearing about a British brushless shaving cream product, they hired a chemist and set out to formulate their own brand. It is said that Burma-Shave was created after forty-three attempts to find a unique and quality product that could be used daily.

To promote the product, the company began erecting the signs, and sales peaked until 1947. The signs, coveted by many, were not as successful when posted on the newer, faster highways, as motorists raced by with less time to read the verses. In 1963, the company was sold to Gillette, later becoming a part of American Safety Razor and Philip Morris. It was called progress when the company removed the signs nationwide, deeming them a silly marketing scheme.

Today, Burma-Shave sign replicas appear along the Mother Road, sponsored by museums or visitor bureaus. They are as much a nostalgic sight along the highway as the retro diners, renovated gas stations and neon-clad motels. Original signs are coveted by museums and collectors and are proudly displayed, to the delight of the public.

A book titled *Verse by the Side of the Road*, by Frank Rowsome Jr., archived the many jingles erected over the decades, and some are available on the Internet. The book is available at Amazon.com. A typical sign from 1932 promotes the product:

Lawyers, doctors
Sheiks and bakers
Mountaineers and undertakers
Make their bristly beards behave
By using brushless
Burma-Shave

Other rhymes promoted safe driving:

You can't reach 80
Hale and hearty
By driving 80
Home from the party
Burma-Shave

And others were just plain silly:

No, no
She said
To her bristly beau
I'd rather
Eat the mistletoe
Burma-Shave

The brand may have disappeared, but the advertising has remained a favorite memory for those who traveled the highways between 1925 and 1966.

AZUSA: GOODBYE FOOTHILL DRIVE-IN

Windows began to fill with steam as couples huddled in their classic cars. Onscreen, Steve McQueen was begging the authorities to do something about the giant blob that was devouring all in its way. It was "goodbye" night at the Foothill Drive-In in Azusa, mourning its impending demise and ending decades of movie entertainment on this section of Route 66. The event was sponsored by Duarte's public access channel, DCTV, and other nonprofit organizations in June 2001.

Opened in 1961, the drive-in was a favorite date destination for more than forty years until it went the way of many Route 66 icons, relegated to history. The Foothill was the last drive-in theater on the route west of Oklahoma City. Ousted by adjacent Azusa Pacific College, the site is now a parking lot, although the famed marquee, after pleas from preservation groups, remains. The giant screen was removed in 2005. The signage is now a historic California landmark.

The city of Azusa boasts a colorful history from the time of the Gabrielino Indians to the land grant of Luis Arena, who sold his

The Foothill Drive-In marquee is all that remains of the Route 66 icon in Azusa. In June 2001, several local organizations bade farewell to the drive-in with a goodbye party that featured a showing of *The Blob.* Decades of family entertainment ceased that night.

holdings to Henry Dalton in 1845. The discovery of gold created an exciting chapter in Azusa history, and eventually another sort of gold was discovered: travelers along the Mother Road, spawning the need for local services such as motels, cafés and garages. Although the city has modernized, some of the vestiges of its Route 66 days remain.

The historic Wells Fargo Bank Building at Route 66 and Azusa Avenue stands today. Next door is Leo C. Nasser's men's clothing store, which is a Route 66 original, as is evident in the old glass bricks and neon signs. The historic Bright Spot Tavern, a Mother Road icon, was preserved, now dubbed Corky's Place. The Stardust and Colonial Motels remain as reminders of the days travelers from the East sought a meal and bed after a tough day of driving.

Azusa City Hall, completed in 1928, is on the National Register of Historic Places. Although the town's name has been said to be a reference to "everything from A to Z in the USA," it is more likely that the name is derived from the Tongva word *Asuksagna*.

Known as "the Canyon City," Azusa marks the gateway to the Angeles National Forest and is nestled below the gaping quarry scar. It is flanked on the west by the San Gabriel River, a border that inexplicably spreads north, above Duarte's Fish Canyon.

Route 66 motorists crossed the San Gabriel River via a concrete tee bridge built in 1922 and rehabilitated in 1947. The span is anchored on the east in Irwindale and on the west in Azusa on the border of Duarte. It must have been a shocking scene to Route 66 motorists traversing the bridge during the great floods of 1938. Although the Foothill bridge was not compromised, the 1907 Puente Largo bridge only yards to the north partially collapsed. That bridge was one of the last legs of the Pacific Electric Railway, carrying the "Red Cars" over the river. Although the bridge was renovated several years ago, the base portions of the wooden poles, which carried the electric car wires, were left intact for the sake of history.

Preserving the Mother Road

Route 66 was the Mother Road of hopes and dreams and of fun and adventure. It embodied the spirit of a nation on the move. With this poignant description at its core, the Route 66 Preservation Foundation is actively working toward developing resources for the preservation and benefit of the Route 66 corridor and its community.

The foundation looks to preserve the route in all eight states. Working alongside is the California Route 66 Preservation Foundation, which is concentrating on California's stretch of the highway.

Both foundations aim to build a higher level of public visibility and awareness throughout the state, the nation and the world and to distribute new resources to worthy, qualified organizations that share its vision.

In addition, the National Park Service has created the Route 66 Corridor Preservation Program, which provides funding assistance in the form of cost-share grants to support the preservation of the most significant and representative historic Route 66 buildings, structures, road segments and cultural landscapes in the eight states through which the route passes. Also, assistance is provided to support research, planning, oral history and education outreach projects related to the preservation of Route 66. This year, a total of more than $83,000 was awarded for five projects.

Preservation of the Mother Road is also the focus of another group, the Route 66 Alliance, which seeks to preserve about 2.4 million acres of the Mojave Desert in southeastern San Bernardino County.

In addition to efforts to preserve structures, signs and actual portions of the original Route 66 roadway, there are those striving to document and preserve the memories of persons who traversed the road in its early days. "We are working with a consortium of archives across the route to encourage the safeguarding of historic Route 66 journals, photos and maps so that people can see and learn from them for generations to come," says Kaisa Barthuli of the Route 66 Preservation Program, National Park Service. In California, the Autry National Center, Museum of the National West, serves as a repository where such journals are preserved.

Will these combined preservation efforts lead to a Mother Road National Monument? Perhaps. With all of the organizations striving to save the spirit of the Mother Road, whether by preserving its memories or encouraging the preservation of its physical icons, California may lead the way in protecting the integrity of the famed highway.

Part V
Duarte to Santa Monica

Duarte: The End of the Trails

Route 66 icons graced the Mother Road through Duarte for decades, but sadly, most have vanished, victims of a philosophy that newer is better.

A favorite hangout and steakhouse for locals and travelers alike, the Trails Restaurant (1952–2001), was an eatery that "started small but vigorous in 1952 on riverbank land acquired in unincorporated territory along a two lane road known as Route 66. A welcome stop for travelers, it earned a reputation for serving hefty portions, thick soups, crusty cheese bread and lounge entertainment."

The community was shocked in 2001 when the owners closed the restaurant. No one was more surprised than Sylvia Price, seventy-two years old at the time of the closing. She began waitressing at the Trails in her twenties and learned of the sale only when she arrived for her shift and found the doors closed. Today a plaque, surrounded by a sea of homes, stands in tribute to the former restaurant. The Trails' back bar is in use at the Continental Room in Fullerton, and the wagon wheel chandelier, signs, a menu and other memorabilia are on exhibit at the Victorville Route 66 Museum.

The Blvd. Café, which stood on the Route where the Ralphs Plaza now stands, was one of Duarte's most treasured icons. Founded in 1946 by the late Susie and Tommy Tomasian, it was passed on to their children and flourished for years as a popular hangout. Known for its chili and "really

A cozy bar, organ music and sizzling steaks served with crusty cheese bread and tureens of soup were only a few of the draws to the Trails Restaurant along the route in Duarte. It remained a favorite Mother Road restaurant from its opening in 1952 until it was sold to a developer in 2001, much to the surprise of not only the patrons but the employees as well.

messy hamburgers," the café was frequented by movie stars such as Red Skelton. The iconic Blvd. Café sign is on display at the California Route 66 Museum in Barstow. Duarte's Big Sky Drive-In was demolished to make room for the former Gemco Plaza on Route 66 east of Mountain, now the Target Plaza.

In easternmost Duarte, on the north side of Huntington Drive, stands a concrete cast building decorated with river rock that serves as "Wepackitall." Built by the O.K. Earl Company in 1965 as a distribution center for British-made motorcycles, it was visited by Lord Snowdon when he accompanied Princess Margaret on a visit to the area. A plaque on the building is still intact.

Dozens of Route 66 motels that flourished during the route's glory days have vanished. The completion of the 210 Freeway spelled doom for many traveler services, one of which was the Evergreen Motel. The mission-style house was designed by architect John C. Austin, who also designed the Griffith Observatory and Los Angeles City Hall. Built in 1921 as a home, it was later a sanitarium and then, to meet the needs of Route 66 travelers, became a motel. It was demolished by the city, leaving an empty lot to the present time.

Among the other vanished icons are Honeyville, Calvert's Soft Drinks, Crystals Café (now Cabreras), the Zanzibar, the Way It Was, the Columbia Bowl and Randall's gas station.

In a grass-roots effort organized by a committee of volunteers, Duarte has sponsored a parade each September to salute its Route 66 heritage. The first parade, held in 1996, featured as its grand marshal the late Bobby Troup, composer of the song "(Get Your Kicks on) Route 66."

Though most physical icons along the road have vanished, the spirit of the route remains through the annual parade. Many businesses along the road incorporate Route 66 into their names, such as the Route 66 Roadhouse and the Route 66 Car Wash.

The Desbrow Journal: A Historical Account

What was it like to travel Route 66 in its fledgling years? Fortunately, it was not unusual for those brave enough to attempt the trip to document their experiences, allowing a window into their personal observations during a challenging era. These journals provide a nostalgic firsthand account of the hardships endured and the frequent encounters with inclement weather, lack of facilities, mechanical breakdowns and sheer exhaustion from negotiating a road fraught with obstacles.

Marilyn Desbrow, a resident of La Puente, says, "When my mother-in-law [Mary] died about twenty years ago, we found the most interesting account in her belongings of a trip she and her husband made from Los Angeles to Chicago on Route 66 in 1930. With two small children, one very sick, they encountered many hardships along the way. Storms, car trouble and a bout of measles did not deter them from their goal."

The journal starts in Los Angeles in March: "Had 74 dollars. Bought gas in Alhambra for $1.05 and two tires for $4." Traveling through the California desert, she wrote, "This is all desert—few houses. Got puncture in tire. Tube was no good so we bought one for 75 cents. Awfully windy. Passed Ludlow about 3 p.m.…Got to Siberia, a nice place." They ventured through Bagdad and on to Needles, where they encountered a storm. "Its a nice little town, right on the Colorado River."

The family stayed in camps, often sleeping outside. Typically, when it rained, they slept in cabins. She wrote, "for $1.25, one room, bed, mattress, wood stove, table and two chairs." They were thrilled to see "prehistoric Indian caves," were stopped by the authorities "to see if we had fruit" and mailed postcards home from Hackberry, Arizona. They passed through Williams, picking up two young men in Peach Springs who needed a ride.

"Passed through Flagstaff, Winslow, Holbrook and Navajo and stayed in Albuquerque," she noted, adding that "we had little pavement in Gallup, the 13 miles on the west side was rough." On they went to Moriarty and Fort Sumter, where they slept in a free camp.

Reaching Texas, they camped behind a gas station. Amarillo, she noted, "is a big town." They picked up groceries and "a new gasket in Texola, Oklahoma. Four exhaust valves almost burned out so we have to buy new ones and do 'em again." They left Galena, Kansas, and drove to Joplin, Missouri, where "they have traffic signals on every corner." Paying twenty-five cents for a tent space, they moved into the car to sleep when a rainstorm hit. In Springfield, Missouri, "we got our rear-end greased."

"We are going to cross the Mississippi soon to get to Illinois State…At night we put our bed up…it gets windy and turns to cyclone. Some states get lots of damage."

After arriving in Chicago, the family settled in for a new life, but when winter came, they longed to return to California. On June 8, 1931, an entry cited: "Baby born at 11:56 p.m. We named him Richard Alfred." This new baby grew up to be Marilyn's husband, now deceased. Mary wrote: "A nurse…stays with me for one week. Monday the 17th sister gets sick and next day Bobby, with Scarlet Fever…I'll be glad when we leave this town."

The family returned to California, leaving Chicago on August 31. Her journal read: "We sure had some bad roads today. 25 miles from Gallup the trailer tire went flat. We stayed at White's Cottage Camp on highway 666." Serving the four corners area, Highway 666, then called the "Devil's Highway," was renamed Highway 491 in 2003. Not only did it have the satanic connotation with the original designation, but traffic fatalities were also high.

The journal, written by Mary Desbrow, was handwritten, and the contents later typed by one of her teenage sons. Marilyn donated a copy of the journal to the National Park Service Route 66 Preservation Program repository at the Autry National Center.

Monrovia: Home of the Aztec

Monrovia's stretch of Route 66 is punctuated with the unique Aztec Hotel, a famed and popular icon that stands out among other memorable Mother Road gems in this all-American city.

Route 66 through Duarte is now named Huntington Drive, and after traveling a few blocks west across the Monrovia border, the early route

Built in the 1920s, the charming Aztec Hotel is a classic on the California highway, allowing patrons to recapture the ambience of the route's glory days. The owner has struggled to keep it functioning. It is on the National Register of Historic Places.

curves to the north on Shamrock, and almost immediately a photo op appears: a classic-style gas station with vintage gas pumps. It is said that a movie about the Lindbergh kidnapping was filmed here. A bit north, lined with craftsman homes, the early route turns west as Foothill Boulevard.

At Magnolia Avenue, the charming Aztec Hotel, a classic of the old California highway, stands out on this original portion of the route. It was built in the 1920s by colorful architect Robert Stacy-Judd, whose creations were inspired by Mayan and Aztec influences. This restored hotel is on the National Register of Historic Places and boasts an ornate lobby, a banquet room and a patio. The Elephant Bar and Restaurant is unique, with brass railings, stained glass and antique lighted ceiling fans that spin from a single belt drive. Here you can capture the ambience of the route's glory days while relaxing with a drink or meal.

At the western stretch of the early route, a number of vintage motor courts exist, including the 1921 Harding Court, composed of fifteen bungalows designated as a historic landmark.

To follow the later alignment of Route 66, continue west on Huntington Drive rather than turning north on Shamrock. On this portion of the route, the 1940 landmark Pottery Ranch stands out as another road icon. Today, it perpetually advertises a "closing out sale" but continues in operation with its vintage neon sign.

Monrovia is where Dick and Mac McDonald opened their first hot dog stand, which they called the Airdrome, across from what was the Monrovia Airport. The hot dog stand was, of course, the venture that grew into today's chain of McDonald's fast-food restaurants.

For route travelers, the presence of old and new routes, realignments and bypasses can be very confusing. After the road was dedicated, it underwent many improvements and reroutings, as faster and more direct roads were incorporated into its existence. The route was officially established in November 1926, but the signs were not installed until the following year. Some bypasses were adopted to circumvent congestion, often over the opposition of nearby towns that stood to lose business as a result.

To accurately find your way through old and new alignments and bypass routes in the San Gabriel Valley, check with the maps in current guidebooks: *Finding the End of the Mother Road: Route 66 in Los Angeles County*, by Scott R. Piotrowski; *Guide to Historic Route 66 in California*, published by the California Historic Route 66 Association; and *EZ 66 Guide for Travelers*, by Jerry McClanahan.

A Road Surrounded by Fact and Myth

More than any other highway, Route 66 is shrouded in myth and mystery, dreams and nightmares, successes and failures. Those who traveled the road, as well as those who lived along its path, were forever changed in its wake.

Researching the history of America's Highway is an enlightening project that comes with a challenge: separating fact from myth. As the years pass, memories fade and stories about the route become murky.

Did Sammy Davis Jr. really lose his eye on the road? Who termed the highway "the Road of Flight" and exactly how many miles does the road encompass? Many interesting "facts" are repeated in history and guide books.

Historians tell us that the road from Los Angeles to Chicago is 2,448 miles. However, this is not exactly true since there have been many different alignments throughout the years. Current maps do not include Old Route 66 since the last stretch of the road disappeared from official maps in 1984.

The road crosses eight states and three time zones and was not completely paved until 1937. In downtown Albuquerque, Route 66 crosses itself at Central Avenue. Due to a change in alignment, you can stand on the corner of Route 66 and Route 66.

Author John Steinbeck termed Route 66 "the Road of Flight." It is also called the Mother Road, America's Highway, the Avenue of Dreams, the Main Street of America and Will Rogers Highway. In Kingman, it is labeled the Andy Devine Highway. The official Route 66 automobile is the Corvette. The last original Route 66 road sign was taken down in Chicago on January 7, 1977. The oldest hotel on Route 66 is the Eagle Hotel in Wilmington, Illinois. Empty today, the circa 1837 hotel once serviced stagecoach travelers, and there are plans to renovate and reopen it.

The official Route 66 song is "(Get Your Kicks on) Route 66." The story goes that Bobby Troup had already written the hit "Daddy" before he became a marine captain in 1942. Five years later and out of the service, he headed for Hollywood with his wife. Turning onto Route 66 from Highway 40, his wife leaned over and suggested a new song title: "(Get Your Kicks on) Route 66." Instantly captivated, Troup created the tune and presented it to Nat King Cole, who was so enthused he asked to record it right away. Later, Cole told Troup that of all the songs he recorded, this was the most requested.

Only a few scenes of the *Route 66* television series were actually filmed on the route.

Would you believe there is a Czech Route 66 Association? There are Route 66 clubs in many foreign countries, such as Great Britain, France, Germany and Amsterdam.

The Roy Rogers Museum, formerly located near Route 66 in Victorville, closed its doors and reopened in Branson, Missouri. Due to a lack of business, it was soon closed and the contents sold at auction. Roy's 1964 Bonneville was sold for $254,500, Trigger's saddle and bridle for $386,000.

In 1952, Sammy Davis Jr. was returning to Los Angeles from a gig in Las Vegas. He was involved in a car accident at a fork on Route 66 at Cajon Boulevard and Kendall Drive. The crash, which nearly left him dead, did result in the loss of his left eye. He wore a patch for a while and then a glass eye. He continued entertaining until his death in 1990.

In 1928, Andy Hartley Payne, a member of the Cherokee Indian tribe, ran 3,423 miles from Los Angeles to New York City, much of it along Route 66. It took him 573 hours, 4 minutes and 34 seconds, averaging six miles per hour. At the end, he was declared the winner of the so-called Bunion Derby.

These are just a few of the alluring stories and "facts" emanating from the Mother Road. They are basically accepted as fact, with maybe a few disputed twists and turns.

ARCADIA: GAMBLING TOWN OR RURAL HAVEN?

Arcadia, "a place of rural simplicity," is named after a district in Greece and has a wildly diverse Route 66 history. This San Gabriel town was a source of hope during the Great Depression as Route 66 improved

A windmill in Arcadia? This one is what remains from the days that this Denny's Restaurant was known as Van de Kamp's. Located near the Santa Anita racetrack, it remains a popular stop for Route 66 motorists.

and businesses flourished. Its image had improved from the 1800s, when it was condemned by many as "a gambling hell and booze pleasure park, a city with an acclaimed racetrack where saloons and roadhouses outnumbered schools, churches and general stores combined," according to *Arcadia: Where Ranch and City Meet* by Pat McAdam and Sandy Snider.

When the city's image improved, it was a source of hope for those who took to America's Highway to escape the Dust Bowl and poverty.

Located on Old Route 66, Santa Anita Park is the oldest racing facility in Southern California. In 1941, the Japanese attack on Pearl Harbor eventually sparked a drastic change in Arcadia. Japanese residents, citizens or not, were ordered by President Franklin D. Roosevelt to relocate to internment camps. Santa Anita Park was chosen to provide temporary housing for those waiting to be assigned to a camp. The Mother Road, a symbol of hope and deliverance, was for a while the scene of a dark chapter in America's history.

With the wild success of the racetrack, businesses in the area flourished, and dozens of cafés, coffee shops, garages and motels opened to service travelers and racetrack fans. Although those peak days waned when freeways displaced Route 66, Arcadia continued to thrive, and some businesses created in the route's heyday still lure the public today.

Arcadia's Derby Restaurant, opened in 1938 by George Woolf, the jockey who rode Seabiscuit to victory in the "Race of the Century," is a local landmark. Rod's Grill, a 1950s coffee shop, was once threatened with demolition but continues to serve patrons today, and a Dutch-style windmill-topped Denny's at Huntington and Santa Anita was once a Van de Kamp Bakery.

For those intent on following Route 66 through Arcadia and points south and west, confusion reigns as new and old routes exist, muddling hopes of a clear direction. *Finding the End of the Mother Road*, by Scott Piotrowski, is a guide that helps keep Route 66 enthusiasts on track with simple maps and explanations. "Throughout its history, Route 66 saw several incarnations. Where highways may have originally hugged around the side of a hill, later it may have gone straight over the top," wrote Piotrowski. "It traversed several different alignments at various points in time."

Many Route 66 travelers during the 1930s, 1940s and 1950s never reached Arcadia, planting their roots in one of the many towns to the east. For motorists who arrived in Arcadia, the citrus ranches, flourishing businesses and racetrack would have been tempting places to squat. From Rosemead Boulevard, Route 66 becomes Colorado Boulevard through East Pasadena to Pasadena and on to the coast. The end of the highway is in sight.

Bridging the Impassable

Route 66 continues to live up to its reputation as part of the nostalgic saga in American culture, spanning the country's era of travel by car and the explosion of its pop culture to its present yearning for preservation. The creation of America's Main Street allowed motorists to travel from Chicago to Los Angeles on one long and continuous albeit oftentimes primitive road. This feat could not have been accomplished without one important component: the bridge.

Although many of the bridges along the route were constructed of concrete and lack ornamentation, there are notable bridges that remain

Spanning the Mojave River, this bridge in Victorville is but one of the many bridges along the route that connect bank to bank and people to people. Bridges on the route attract history buffs and photographers.

a delight to history buffs and photographers, bridges held in high esteem in the eyes of artists and architects. These links connect riverbank to riverbank, but more importantly, they also connect people to people and allow motorists to cross rivers, gorges and otherwise impassable sections.

Motoring along the Old Route between California to Chicago affords opportunity to stop, enjoy and, of course, photograph a variety of bridges from concrete to steel truss. One outstanding bridge is located in an Arizona town that is hard to forget: Winona. Once instrumental in the flow of traffic along the route, this iron bridge was the victim of neglect and was sadly closed and abandoned, though it is still visible to motorists.

Of the many bridges, there is one that is captivating in its history, architecture and lore. Spanning the great Mississippi River, the mile-long Chain of Rocks Bridge is anchored in Missouri on one end and in Illinois on the other. It is one of the longest steel-truss bridges in the nation and has a twenty-two-degree bend in the middle. Route 66 travelers once forked over a five-cent toll to continue across this 1929 structure. Today, it is reserved for pedestrians and bicycles and offers opportunity for a serene stroll, with magnificent views of the river and surrounding area. It was featured in a scene in the movie *Escape from New York*.

Route 66 crosses a corner of Kansas, a mere thirteen-mile stretch, but along those miles, a charming bridge may be found on the Old Route: the unique and historic Rainbow Bridge, the last of three "Marsh Arch" bridges. A single-span concrete bridge, it is the last of this type of bridge along the former highway. It is on the National Register of Historic Places.

Another great old steel-truss bridge is a Route 66 structure built in 1930 that crosses the Mojave River just outside Victorville near Oro Grande. When traveling the Sagebrush Annie portion of the highway from Barstow to Victorville, this bridge is a bonus after a thirty-mile road rife with nostalgic icons.

The famed Colorado Street Bridge in Pasadena is less known for its graceful lines and curve than for its reputation as "Suicide Bridge." This concrete arch bridge that spans the Arroyo Seco was built in 1913, is on the National Register of Historic Places and was declared a National Historic Engineering Landmark. Traffic on the bridge is rerouted annually to allow a festival to be held honoring the bridge's history.

The Victorville Route 66 Museum features a comprehensive photographic history of bridges along Route 66.

PASADENA: THE ENVY OF A NATION

The nation and the world probably know one small strip of Route 66 better than any other section of the road. That stretch is Colorado Boulevard, where the annual Tournament of Roses Parade has marched along since the 1890s. The festivities have grown in grandeur and popularity through the years, while television has delivered Route 66 with its magnificent mountain backdrop right into homes worldwide.

From Arcadia, cross Rosemead Boulevard, and Route 66 becomes Colorado Boulevard through East Pasadena. For motorists attempting to follow America's Highway today, the trip can be frustrating and confusing due to numerous old and new alignments. Fortunately, guide books and maps are available.

See along the way restaurants such as Cameron's, anchored by its large neon fish sign, Jake's of Pasadena and the Rose City Diner touting ambience of years past. Here antique stores abound, as do vintage motels that remain as a testament to a time when travelers were in dire need of shelter and food.

In one alignment, Route 66 follows Colorado Boulevard over the Arroyo Seco across the 1913 Colorado Street Bridge, famous for its graceful curves. Nicknamed "Suicide Bridge," it is said that during the Great Depression numerous individuals jumped from the structure.

Following Colorado Boulevard, the road passes Figueroa Street into Eagle Rock and in 1934 followed what is now Eagle Rock Boulevard. However, the original 1926 route turned south on Fair Oaks Boulevard to Huntington Drive, Mission Road, North Broadway and Sunset Boulevard.

The turn on Fair Oaks Boulevard reveals myriad remnants of the road's heyday leading into South Pasadena. The Fair Oaks Pharmacy and Soda Fountain was in full swing at the dedication of Route 66, having opened in 1915. Located at the corner of Mission and Fair Oaks, it continues to serve its famed fountain drinks. Gus's Barbeque,

Pasadena's "Suicide Bridge" spans the Arroyo Seco. Its nickname stems from the suicide incidents that occurred there during the Great Depression. Of late, traffic is rerouted one day each year when the bridge becomes the site of a festival.

established in 1946, dishes up the juicy ribs, which have attracted customers since that time.

Probably one of the most controversial and photographed sites in the area is the 1925 Rialto Theater, one of the last single-screen movie theaters in Southern California. Will this icon fall victim to the wrecking ball? Not if the many preservationists bent on saving the structure have their way. Only time will tell.

A far cry from the dusty desert towns and the communities along the vanished citrus groves of the San Gabriel Valley, the route west from Pasadena becomes convoluted, rife with traffic and congestion. Even pulling over to take a photo can be problematic. But the icons are there for those who care to search, and the history in the area is rich and colorful. As the route closes in on the City of the Angels, vintage buildings hint at a past era. But first the road cuts through Highland Park, a town surprisingly flush with Route 66 signs and icons.

It is perhaps here where travelers become frustrated with the hustle and bustle of city life. However, the end is in sight as the Will Rogers Highway will soon disappear at the Pacific Coast.

McMAHON TREK PREDATES ROUTE 66

So significant and precious are personal journals written by those who traveled America's highways during the fledgling years of the automobile that a special repository is maintained at the Autry Museum to ensure their preservation. And yet, many such journals are discarded after the author dies, and surviving family members fail to see any relevance in such diaries.

I have been fortunate to receive personal journals recounting travel on Route 66 and like highways during a time when travel was treacherous, dangerous and exhausting. Although automobile technology was rudimentary at best, the mass production of cars gave opportunity for a once rooted society to take to the road. Travelers faced constant breakdowns, and there were large gaps in the availability of gas and water. Whether fleeing the Dust Bowl, searching for better employment opportunities or simply out to see the country, courageous motorists braved the challenge.

Above: The McMahons traveled in this vehicle in 1922 when they drove from Drexel Hill, Pennsylvania, to Santa Barbara. Their journey, which predated Route 66, was filled with adventure along many roads that were barely passable. *Courtesy of the McMahon family.*

Right: Paul and Ruth McMahon in 1921. Their travels across the nation were chronicled in a journal that was preserved by their granddaughter, Carrie McMahon Humphrey, who had the foresight to recognize its importance. *Courtesy of the McMahon family.*

One such poignant account was discovered by Carrie McMahon Humphrey, a Glendora resident for thirty-four years, who typed her grandmother's handwritten account. The journey predates Route 66 and traverses a more northern route, but it eloquently sets forth the challenges facing travelers during that time. Carrie prefaces the journal:

> *This journal is dedicated to the memory of Paul and Ruth McMahon. It chronicles their journey in 1922 from Drexel Hill, Pennsylvania across the Northern United States to Santa Barbara, California and most of their stops along the way. The descriptions are in Grandmother "Ruthie's" own words with photographs by Grandfather Paul. I hope you enjoy reading the journal as much as I did in preparing it.*

The hardships endured were typical of the time and serve to ignite a spark of appreciation for the luxuries motorist enjoy today:

> *We passed through Trenton and Princeton, and at 8 p.m. stopped near New Brunswick, New Jersey where we pitched camp in a field of new-mown hay The mosquitoes were fierce and fortunately for us, the meal in Roxboro proved sufficient to last us until morning, so we lost no time in putting up cots and crawling in under the canopies where we listened to the mosquitoes singing about the netting until we fell asleep.*

Poor road conditions were reported almost daily, such as on August 20, 1922:

> *Left camp 1:30; made 40 miles in the first hour! Concrete, straight, almost no houses; after that gravel-dirt roads. Started to rain quite hard about 3 p.m. All went well till we suddenly struck an all-dirt road which had been well rain soaked, and 100 yards from the place we struck it, we slid gracefully and gently into the ditch. A chap came along who had done the same thing and helped shove us out. We decided to try to push on, and proceeded at about ten miles an hour. Not quite a mile from where we had been ditched, the car started a gentle sideways slide, and we landed with the back wheel in a much deeper ditch than the first one!*

A mile from this occurrence, they once again slid into a ditch but were saved by passersby. "Altogether it took ten men one hour to get us out of the ditch."

At the time of their travels, there was no continuous road to navigate. Each day was an adventure and an exercise in creatively finding ways to overcome obstacles that seemed never ending. On September 7, the journal describes the weather:

> *This was to be our wash day, but we found a strong wind blowing, laden with fine white dust and small particles of sand. It blew harder and harder and soon was a perfect gale. Our breakfast consisted of boiled eggs and cheese sandwiches, generously peppered with dust. Cooking was impossible. It was a horrible day. The sand or dust storm lasted till about four o'clock, and then it stopped and turned bitter cold. We played Fan Tan till supper time, and then spent a very cold night in bed—frost fell as soon as the sun set.*

On October 16, 1922, the McMahons reached their destination, Santa Barbara:

> *Santa Barbara was an ocean drive and we didn't want to miss it. But in the dark, we failed to recognize it as a town and went past—kept looking for signs, all we could see were road construction signs, finally saw sign saying 10 miles to Santa Barbara. Paul said that if anyone asked his impression of scenery between Las Cruces and Santa Barbara, he'd say "Dangerous but Passable!"*

Highland Park: Reuniting on America's Highway

Highland Park covets an abundance of Route 66 icons that are enthusiastically preserved by friends of the road. Located along the Arroyo Seco, it is bordered by the Pasadena Freeway, South Pasadena, Oak Grove Drive and Avenue 50/51. It is said to be one of the oldest settled areas of Los Angeles. Sadly, many of its grandest homes were destroyed during the 1950s and '60s. As a consolation, some of the architecturally significant homes were saved and are on display at Highland Park's Heritage Square. The town's current population is more than fifty-seven thousand.

The Southwest Museum was once touted as the gem of Highland Park. After merging with the Autry Museum of Western Heritage in Griffith Park, the Southwest's public exhibition facilities were closed, a move that has remained a bitter pill to swallow by some. The extensive collection of Native American artifacts was moved to the Autry Museum, with the original Southwest Museum site utilized as a library and research center.

Driving along Figueroa Street, we stop to photograph the icons that once were thriving businesses along the Mother Road. A series of Route 66 road signs mark the way. The Highland Theater, designed by architect L.A. Smith, is marked by its rooftop sign towering against the sky. Still open for business, it has been designated a historic

Chicken Man stands like a sentinel guarding the surrounding city of Highland Park. Standing twenty-two feet high, this fiberglass statue once roosted on Broadway in downtown Los Angeles.

cultural monument and is part of a unique fundraising project that is in full swing. The individual light bulbs composing the sign are up for adoption by a group called Friends of the Historic Signs of Figueroa Street. Also included in the sign renovation program is the 1924 Manning Coffee Store sign.

Nearby stands the quirky, twenty-two-foot-tall Chicken Boy, which is rooted in Los Angeles history. Hatched on a rooftop on a Broadway portion of Route 66, he now roosts in Highland Park. It seems that there is an entire industry dedicated to saving and selling chicken signs!

One of Highland Park's premier Route 66 sites is the beautiful Sycamore Grove Park, a park so long that it merits four freeway off ramps. It was a social site during the 1920s, '30s and '40s, when replanted citizens would hold reunions to reunite with those hailing from their home state and town. These traditional reunions were referred to as "State Society Picnics." For instance, in 1925, dozens of transplants from Nebraska gathered, and in 1926 a reunion for those hailing from Alaska was held. According to Piotrowski's guide, the band shell in Sycamore Grove Park "was a regular venue for John Philip Sousa, who would then stay with his friend, Dr. Hiner, across the street. The Hiner House still stands, as does the band shell."

Route 66 through Highland Park is also called the Arroyo Seco Parkway, and the freeway section is State Route 110 (the Pasadena Freeway). It is a national engineer landmark and a national scenic byway. Here you will find four tunnels, purported to be the only tunnels on the entire Route 66. At the southern end of the Arroyo Seco Parkway is a four-level interchange, said to be the first of its kind in the United States, which unites three freeways.

Saying goodbye to the unique town of Highland Park, Route 66 enters what most people think of as the western gateway to Los Angeles through the famed streets of Hollywood.

A Trip Inside the Earth via 66

Not all Route 66 travelers during the 1930s were fleeing the Dust Bowl or abandoning their homes in search of better opportunities in the West. As automobiles became more reliable and Route 66 underwent improvements, motorists with the means and chutzpah took to America's Highway to see the sights of the nation.

One such destination was a place the Chemehuevis called "the eyes of the mountain," more commonly known as Mitchell Caverns. The caves, located in the Providence Mountains of California's Mojave Desert, became the property of Jack and Ida Mitchell through a series of mining ventures and remained in their care from 1934 to 1954. The couple recognized the tourist potential in this naturally decorated limestone cavern. However, the closest town was Essex on Route 66, some twenty-two miles away.

A determined man, Jack knew what he must do. He forged the primitive prospector's trail leading from the Route 66 town of Essex to the cave into a road good enough for "city folk who had money to spend." Jack became a trailblazer, chopping at plants with a hatchet

This former home of Jack and Ida Mitchell serves as a ranger station at Mitchell Caverns, now owned by the state park system. Some twenty-two miles from the Route 66 town of Essex, travelers could negotiate a road blazed by Mitchell to reach the caverns for a tour.

under the burning desert sun. One day while in town, he met a trucker who was hauling a Caterpillar tractor. Jack was a convincing man, and soon the tractor was at work blazing a road up the mountain.

This was but one of Jack's projects. Tourists would need food, water and maybe a night's stay in addition to a cave tour. A creative couple, the Mitchells made furniture from old auto cushions, cholla and the skeleton heads of sheep. He also appointed himself "a one-man chamber of commerce," advertising his "resort" to attract customers. He had to spread the word that "Essex was a town, not an automobile."

From their porch, the Mitchells enjoyed an unobstructed view across the subtle hues of the vast desert. They would constantly spot dust clouds as visitors drove up the dirt road to visit. Cave tours included the opportunity to see ornate speleothems and to learn about the paleological and archaeological finds in the area. As word spread, Jack and Ida found their abode to be a popular destination for tourists motoring along Route 66.

Jack reportedly escorted more than forty thousand tourists through the caverns over a period of twenty years. Sadly, in 1954, at the age of seventy-two, he died when a car he was working under slipped from the car jack and crushed him. Coincidentally, before his death, in order to preserve the caves and the homestead, he made arrangements for the state park to take over the caverns.

The area became a State Recreation Area in 1956 and now sits in the midst of the East Mojave National Preserve. The visitor center and exhibits are located in what was the Mitchell home, and a half-mile, mostly level trail leads to the cave entrance. State rangers lead groups through about a quarter mile of the cave and narrate the geological and historical significance of the unique limestone caverns.

Route 66 buffs will enjoy what is left of the town of Essex. Here the old pre-1931 alignment of Route 66 rejoins the National Trails Highway and offers picturesque foundations from the town's successful days. From the road, you will see what looks like a wishing well. It is actually a water fountain installed by the Auto Club of Southern California for use by motorists braving the hot summer days along the route.

Note: As this book goes to press, the continuing saga of Mitchell Caverns takes a depressing turn. True to Jack and Ida Mitchell's wishes, California State Park officials have protected the caverns and buildings for eight decades, with guides leading cave tours for a steady stream of tourists. Then, due to budget cuts, the area was closed to the public. Left unguarded, vandals have taken a toll on the visitor center, smashing display cases, doors and windows and making off with gear. Now, a little on the late side, the state is making arrangements to guard the area while it is closed to the public.

MEMORIES OF HOLLYWOOD

Following Route 66 into West Hollywood, everything around me seems familiar. "That was where I had my first job," calls out my husband as we cruise along Sunset Boulevard. As a young teen, he carried dog food orders out to customers waiting in their cars. There is a "V" shape where Sunset and Santa Monica Boulevards meet, a stone's throw from our first apartment on Manzanita Street. I lived on Route 66 and didn't realize it until now.

Hollywood has it all. It is dirty and old, glamorous and exciting, congested and creative, rich in Route 66 history and movie tales. I grew up below the "D" in the HOLLYWOOD sign and walked more than two miles to Hollywood High School each day. Later, I worked as an usherette at the Grauman's Chinese Theater during *Westside Story*, where I had the thrill of escorting Charlton Heston to his seat. I met my husband on a bus stop at the corner of Hollywood and Vine when we were fifteen years old. Clearly, this Route 66 neighborhood feels like home.

We pass Taix French Restaurant on Sunset at the corner of Park. The Taix family immigrated from the "Hautes-Alps from southeastern France in around 1870." In 1912, Mariu Taix opened a hotel in Los Angeles' French Quarter and, later, a restaurant in the hotel. The current Taix Restaurant on Route 66 was opened in 1962 and continues to be operated as a fine dining restaurant. This is where my father would take the family on very special occasions.

Claiming such famous past patrons as Elvis Presley, Howard Hughes, Clark Gable and Lana Turner, the Route 66 Formosa Café is located on Santa Monica Boulevard. At one time, it was threatened to be razed to make way for a Warner Bros. studio parking lot. History buffs united, and their protest in the form of a petition signed by more than two thousand Friends of the Formosa finally prevailed. Opened in 1925, the Formosa

Opened in 1920, Barney's Beanery remains today a favorite haunt on the Mother Road. Stories about the past escapades at the eatery involve such stars as Jimi Hendrix, Janis Joplin and Jim Morrison.

gained fame more for its location than its food. Next door to the Warner Hollywood Studio, it was a favorite haunt for stars and boasts a colorful history with an impressive list of customers even today.

Further west is the Route 66 icon Barney's Beanery, which claims to be a destination for westbound Mother Road travelers of yesterday and today. Opened in 1920, it "evolved into an epicenter for arts and culture in the mid-sixties." I remember it as a rowdy bar scene during the 1970s, with blush-provoking graffiti on the restroom walls. Did Janis Joplon have her last drink there? Did Jim Morrison get ejected for urinating on the bar? True or not, these are stories that attach themselves to this famed restaurant and bar, which is also revered for its famed chili.

Still visible along the route are Hollywood Star Lanes, a 1950s bowling alley, and the Hollywood Memorial Cemetery.

Entering Beverly Hills, the funk subsides and swank prevails. Cement gives way to sprawling lawns, and ornate squatty historic buildings are replaced by the modern sweeping lines of skyscrapers along the Avenue of the Stars. The melting pot of anonymous residents disappears as hawkers sell maps to the homes of the rich and famous living within 90210.

The route crosses Rodeo Drive, and at Wilshire, the atmosphere turns Polynesian with Trader Vic's. Located within the Beverly Hilton Hotel, Trader Vic's is said to be the last remaining tiki bar on Route 66, dating back to 1955.

Traveling west, one wonders if the scent of the ocean is real or imaginary. For Route 66 travelers who remained on the road at this point, the end was imminent, though many had found roots long before closing in on the last miles of the historic highway.

A Road of Many Names

Route 66 has been called many names, some of which were probably not very flattering when the original road was largely unpaved and in bad shape. Over the years, it became more than just a strip of asphalt for autos as it took on a mystical aura and blossomed into a symbol of freedom and hope.

When the U.S. highway system was born, there was controversy over how to assign numbers to interstate roads. Route 66 was one of the first U.S. highways, signed into law in 1927 but not completely paved until 1938. There was talk of officially assigning it Highway 60 or 62, but in the end, it became Highway 66, which was thought to be an easy number to remember and "pleasant to say or hear." After a few decades, the highway's number would also prove to be pleasant to sing about!

Shortly after the road was commissioned, it was given the nickname "the Great Diagonal Way" because the Chicago-to-Oklahoma portion of the road ran northeast to southwest. And later, another moniker took over, one that continues today: the "Main Street of America."

During the 1930s, routed from their homes and farms by the decade-long natural disaster of the Dust Bowl, families saw Route 66 as their only hope for survival. Loading what they could into the family car, they bravely traveled west in hopes of finding a new life. At the same time, in the midst of the Great Depression, thousands of desperate unemployed men headed out on Route 66 with dreams of finding employment in the West. The highway was termed the "Road of Flight" and the "Mother Road" by author John Steinbeck in his famed classic *The Grapes of Wrath.*

In 1952, the U.S. Highway 66 Association unofficially named Route 66 the Will Rogers Highway. Just as the road took on many monikers and descriptions, Will Rogers (William Penn Adair Rogers) wore many hats, such as humorist, cowboy, comedian, social commentator, vaudeville performer and actor. He was appointed goodwill ambassador to Mexico and at one time served briefly as mayor of Beverly Hills. Why was the road named for him? Perhaps it was just a natural consequence of the time when he was so popular. His name is also attached to many parks, a beach, schools, libraries and even a navy submarine!

In Kingman, Arizona, Route 66 is named the Andy Devine Highway. Originally a silent film star, Devine later appeared in "talkies" and was noted for his raspy voice, the result of an accident at an early age. He appeared with John Wayne in movies, and the two remained friends for life. Devine moved to Kingman at the age of thirty-six, and thanks to his hometown fans, Route 66 was named after him. Andy Devine Day is celebrated annually in town. It is said he was actively involved in the Good Roads Association, a group of citizens successful in the National Old Trails Highway following the northern rather than southern route through Phoenix. This highway later became Route 66.

In 1985, the famed road suffered the ultimate insult as it was decommissioned and deemed "no longer relevant," replaced by the U.S. highway system. Portions of the road are designated national scenic byways, and today much of the road is marked by retro "Route 66" signs, as well as giant Route 66 stencils.

As for Route 66, those who dismissed the road as "no longer relevant" have been proven wrong. It is perhaps more relevant today than in its heyday. Its nostalgic aura attracts tourists from around the world, stimulates renovation of enterprises thought obsolete and encourages motorists to once more take to the road in a slower and more relaxed manner. It is a happy and positive story of rebirth. Route 66 books, guides, clothing and memorabilia abound. It is the highway that refuses to die.

ROUTE 66 MEETS THE SEA

From the dusty desert town of Needles through the congestion and confinement of West Hollywood, Route 66 makes its way to the sea. The last alignment of the Mother Road, Santa Monica Boulevard travels through Hollywood, West Hollywood and Beverly Hills. The pre-1939 alignment once ended in downtown Los Angeles but was changed to end in Santa Monica.

Stories abound as to how Santa Monica received its name. Some say it is named to honor the feast day of Santa Monica, while others believe it was named for a spring that dripped water resembling the tears of a crying saint. The town was incorporated in 1886.

Santa Monica has enjoyed periods of prosperity, and it has suffered times when its future was questionable. In the 1930s, gambling ships would anchor offshore, just beyond the legal three-mile limit. Ferried from shore, gamblers enjoyed such ships as the *Rex*, which was launched in 1938. It is said that the *Rex* could accommodate three thousand gamblers at a time. When a court order demanded that the gambling cease, the crew fought off the police with cannons and submachine guns. It took nine days for the ship to surrender, ending the so-called Battle of Santa Monica Bay.

In better times, the sunny sands of the beach attracted crowds, and the Pacific Electric Railway provided ample transportation. Amusement

Although Route 66 originally ended in Los Angeles, it was later extended to the Pacific Ocean at Santa Monica. The pier marks the road's end for today's travelers.

piers became the preferred form of entertainment, and at one time, there were five such piers in Santa Monica alone and more in surrounding beach areas.

During the 1920s, the city of Santa Monica enjoyed growing prosperity, with an increase in population and the establishment of large companies such as Douglas Aircraft, founded in 1921. Construction projects flourished, and elegant resorts appeared, such as the Miramar Hotel, built in 1925. The previous year saw the opening of the La Monica Ballroom on the pier, a venue that could support five thousand partners on the dance floor.

Reaching the coast today is somewhat frustrating due to crowds, congestion and lack of convenient parking. But imagine the delight greeting Route 66 travelers of days gone by. After traveling the road, some for 2,400 or more miles, risking the obstacles rampant in crossing the Mojave Desert, driving through the ranches and orchards of the San Gabriel Valley and then, finally, arriving at the vast, shining waters of the Pacific Ocean. For many travelers, this was the first time they had laid eyes on an ocean, a thrill for adults and children alike.

On the palm-lined grassy bluff just north of the pier, a small information kiosk sells memorabilia and offers information. On the wall, a large sign declares "End of Route 66."

However, it seems these days that the route will never end. In fact, it has become as popular today as it was in its heyday, this time for its historic importance rather than its utilitarian purpose.

Part VI
On the Highway to Chicago

The Big Step: A Monumental Journey

Imagine leaving home, a place where your family roots had spread for generations, loading your children and valuables into a less-than-reliable family car and heading west on a road that was passable only in spots. In the 1920s, '30s and '40s, thousands of families did just that. Fleeing the creeping shadow of poverty, they believed that following the road of hope called Route 66 would deliver them to California, a land of riches, gainful employment and opportunities galore. In reality, even if the trip went well, the promises were often elusive or nonexistent.

We did the opposite. Having retired from well-paying professional jobs, my husband, Alan, and I abandoned for a time the luxuries of home, friends and security to travel decommissioned Route 66 east to Chicago, not such a monumental undertaking today, and yet, rather daunting in a time of economic and security flux. In my SUV, with an eighteen-foot trailer in tow, we set out to explore the towns along the way, meet the peoples of America's heartland and hopefully emerge from the adventure with a better understanding of why the Mother Road transcends its asphalt core, beckoning travelers to forego larger and faster modern highways in search of some sort of epiphany.

Since we had explored the road across the Golden State, we officially began our cross-country trek in Needles with no particular time constraints. Our aim was simply to journey on Route 66 with a few side trips to places we could not fathom missing, such as Santa Fe and Roswell, New Mexico. Armed with a pile of guidebooks and maps, as well as advice from such Route 66 gurus as Jim Hinckley and Jim Conkle, the good folks at the California Route 66 Museum in Barstow and the California Route 66 Mother Road Museum in Victorville, it was "Chicago or bust!" How have towns along the route survived, what remnants of the road's heyday remain and do creative minds continue to lure travelers with quirky and odd attractions? Will people act friendly and forthcoming, or will they be suspicious and resentful?

The challenges we faced were many. First, we must slow down. Flying at seventy miles per hour is unsafe with a trailer in tow, although it is legal in most states. Can we live in such a small space for two months? Will paying bills, writing articles and keeping in touch with family and friends on the Internet work? And then there are the unexpected obstacles, such as inclement weather like tornados and hurricanes, traffic accidents, the price of gas, car repairs and emergencies at home. Will we suffer from an overabundance of togetherness? Can we survive a drastic drop in earnings? These are challenges that we would meet head on.

This whole crazy idea to travel the route came by way of an acquaintance who, in the year of his sixty-sixth birthday, took off in his Mustang and traveled the Mother Road solo. His accounting of the trip was mesmerizing, and we decided that when we turned sixty-six years of age, we would follow the road as well.

That time had arrived, and soon we would embark on our journey. In the next sections, we explore some of the guides and books that are helpful on a Route 66 trek, and then we will travel with Kim Anderson on his adventure exploring America's Highway in 2003. After that, we will head out on our own adventure following the road to Chicago.

GUIDING YOUR WAY ON AMERICA'S HIGHWAY

If you plan to travel west, take the guidebook that's the best. No matter which way you travel on the Mother Road, there are a number of excellent maps and guidebooks that will help plan the trip.

The EZ Route 66 Guide for Travelers, written by Jerry McClanahan and published by the National Historic Route 66 Federation, is not only informative in its maps and descriptions but will also make your trip more fun. There are free updates online. It contains a map that takes you mile by mile along the route, including mileage counts, attractions, historic details and directions. There are alerts to memorable finds and even a scavenger hunt along the way. It is complete yet concise, serious yet fun. The spiral binding makes page turning easy.

Expanding on the Route 66 experience is a new publication, *Keeping You on the Mother Road*, by Dave Emerson. Need a beauty salon, an RV repair garage, an antique dealer or a restaurant? This book promises the answers. "In my book I use custom-made maps and photographs," says Emerson, who is obviously smitten with America's Highway. He spent seven years preparing this guide.

For stories told with flair, you can't beat the writings of Jim Hinckley, author of several Route 66 books, including *Ghost Towns of the Southwest*, *Route 66 Backroads* and *Backroads of Arizona.* His latest book, *Ghost Towns of Route 66*, adds a new dimension to Route 66 exploration. "Through my travels and study of the road, I began to link a forgotten era with the highway, which led to seeing ghosts of Route 66," says Hinckley, who lives along the route in Kingman.

To immerse yourself in the aura of the road and its link with history, reread John Steinbeck's *The Grapes of Wrath* and its poignant descriptions of the horrors facing families traveling west during the Great Depression. A DVD of Ford's film is also available.

Joe De Kehoe's *The Silence and the Sun* is a "historical account of people, places and events on Old Route 66 and railroad communities in the Eastern Mojave Desert." Through detailed interviews, De Kehoe pens a personal account of those who settled in these dusty little towns. His writings compel the reader to journey to the sites, many of which have melded into the earth. Kicking around the abandoned ruins and stone foundations, one can't help but imagine what life was once like in this nearly forgotten land.

The fickle path through Los Angeles to the coast is probably the most confusing section of Route 66. With byways, bypasses, freeways and old and new alignments, confusion reigns. To help sort it out, Scott Piotrowski's *Finding the End of the Mother Road* is a must.

Books on California's portion of the road include the *Guide to Historic Route 66 in California*, now in its third edition, published by the California

Historic Route 66 Association. There is also an Arcadia Publishing work, *Images of America: Route 66 in California*, by Glen Duncan and the California Route 66 Preservation Foundation available.

Kim Anderson's Sixty-sixth Birthday Trek

For years, it was his dream, his passion and his hobby. Kim Anderson, born and raised in Monrovia, California, could be counted as one of the San Gabriel Valley's most dedicated Route 66 fans. He collected vintage postcards, researched hotels and motels of the Mother Road, studied the highway's history and planned for the day that arrived on August 11, 2003. Having reached his sixty-sixth birthday, Anderson took off in his 1996 Mustang for a solo drive the length of Route 66. His goal was to photograph the old, abandoned filling stations and motels and capture the essence of a more innocent and relaxed time.

Anderson's journey took him to scores of nostalgic Route 66 stops, the first a stay at the Beale Hotel in Kingman, Arizona, that boasts such colorful past guests as Charles Lindbergh. He visited the nearby Route 66 Powerhouse Museum, one of the dozens of museums along his way.

Having once served on a local committee researching Monrovia's town clock (located in front of Boxx Jewelers), Anderson took an interest in these once-popular timepieces. He therefore added town clocks to his quests. "I also photographed all the old, deserted and rusted automobiles visible from the highway and sought to snap photos of the hotels remaining from my postcard collection, or at least the location where they once stood," says Anderson.

Documenting and photographing remnants of the numerous filling stations kept Anderson busy. Every day, he would stop at a Dairy Queen for a real chocolate milkshake, "the kind you just can't find in California."

Not alone in his quest, Anderson met dozens of Route 66 buffs indulging in the same experience he was seeking. "I met many travelers from France and Germany traveling along the Mother Road," he said.

Generally enjoying good weather, he recalled a few exceptions, such as summer rainstorms in Flagstaff and Gallup, and record-breaking heat in St. Louis. This validated his decision to drive the road in his Mustang rather than his 1951 Ford Victoria, which he bought new when he was a student at Monrovia-Arcadia-Duarte (MAD) High School.

Besides the sweltering heat in St. Louis, his attempt to complete his journey at the Mother Road's end was stymied by frustrating traffic jams and lack of parking due to a street festival. After traveling 2,400 miles, he was ready to start home.

Anderson's experience is a modern-day example of man seeking to fulfill a dream by traveling the nostalgic Main Street of America. In its heyday, the Mother Road brought visionaries west to what they hoped would be a better life. Today, it links travelers with America's history, fueling a movement throughout the country to preserve the road's icons and to once more beckon those yearning for adventure.

Arizona: Land of Diversity

It was "Chicago or bust" on Route 66 as we towed our trailer over the state border at Needles. Arizona has promoted the Mother Road for more than eighty years. Its tourist literature on the road recognizes its role "in inspiring writers, film-makers, photographers and artists" and describes the route as "a road that represents family road trips, neon, classic cars, cowboys, diners and ever-changing wonders from towering red cliffs, open spaces with endless blue skies."

America's Highway merges in and out of I-40, taking travelers through a multitude of retro small towns decked out in neon. However, in great contrast, there are long stretches of wide-open spaces, distant mesas and striking natural landmarks such as the Painted Desert, the Meteor Crater and the Petrified Forest. A few miles before Kingman, Area 66 (of the "close encounter" kind) beckoned us to exit from the Route 66 realignment at Alamo Road in Yucca to photograph what appeared to be a giant silver golf ball. It is the Dinesphere, a geodesic dome built in 1972 as a restaurant/nightclub. At its base is a small store, which was manned by the owner's visiting son, John, from Glendale, California. Jerky, out-of-this-world memorabilia and doodads are for sale.

From Area 66, we followed Route 66 into Kingman for a stop at the Powerhouse Route 66 Museum. This portion of the Mother Road is named for Andy Devine in honor of the old-time actor. The

Near Kingman on a Route 66 realignment, what looks like a giant golf ball dominates the area. It is the Area 66 Dinosphere, built in 1972 as a restaurant/night club. Today, you can visit the small store, which sells trinkets and jerky.

museum offers information on the trip ahead and features a shop with memorabilia galore. Across the street is Mr. D'z Route 66 Diner, an eatery and photo stop. Jim Hinckley, author of several books on the Mother Road, offered us some travel tips. Hinckley is currently active in restoring Route 66 nostalgia to Kingman. "So much has been lost," he says, "but we are trying to restore what we can such as the neon signs which many establishments once showcased."

East of Kingman, Route 66 winds through Hackberry and its famed iconic Hackberry General Store. Take a peek into the men's room, if you dare. From there, we journeyed through Peach Springs, stopping in Seligman, home of the Road Kill Café, retro diners and dozens of Route 66 souvenir shops. Route 66 in Seligman resembles an outdoor museum, lined with vintage autos, mannequins in hot rods, looming cutouts of Elvis Presley and Marilyn Monroe, motorcycles and neon signs. My favorite stop is the Route 66 Visitor Center, formerly the barbershop. Angel Delgadillo, retired town barber, was home resting when we arrived, but his brother, Joe, ninety, greeted us. Angel received

Route 66 appears to be an outdoor museum as a constant stream of Mother Road buffs visit this once flourishing town. Memorabilia stores abound.

his diploma on December 5, 1947, at the America Barber College in Pasadena. He is the founder of the Arizona Route 66 Association.

Beyond Seligman is Williams, the last Route 66 town bypassed, on October 13, 1984. Here we visited the western-style Railway Hotel, designed to resemble the century-old train depot that housed the original Fray Marcos Hotel opened by the Santa Fe Railroad as a Harvey House. At the depot, a vintage train headed for the Grand Canyon. Neon Burma-Shave signs and mom and pop cafés line the road, reminding us of the days before fast food.

Finishing up a long day of Route 66 sightseeing, we settled into a trailer park across the street from Little America in Flagstaff and dined at Black Bart's Steakhouse and Saloon, where the wait staff sings opera on stage. We found ourselves surrounded by people like us, post-retirement, AARP card–carrying seniors out to experience America.

VISITING NAVAJO COUNTRY

Continuing on, we followed the Highway of Dreams east from Flagstaff, where 66 merges with I-40 in most areas. Whenever possible, we turned onto the Old Road, enjoying a slower pace and making stops at the multitude of rock shops and trading posts.

Not forgetting Winona, we stopped to photograph the town's old truss bridge, which is on the National Register of Historic Places, then continued on to Winslow of Eagles' tune fame. Here, tourists pose in front of a mural of a "girl in a flatbed Ford," next to a statue dedicated to the Eagles.

Here is one of the road's most famous and charming hotels, the La Posada, built in 1928 and designated as a national historic landmark. It is a former Harvey House and was designed by architect Mary Jane Colter. The eclectic art collections, comfy sitting rooms and gardens, the

The 1928 La Posada Hotel in Winslow is one of the road's most famous and charming spots. It is designated as a national historic landmark. Its famed Turquoise Room restaurant and eclectic art attract international guests.

Turquoise Room restaurant and the gift shop attract visitors from all over the world. The moderately priced rooms are delightful and open with what resembles a jail cell key. A favorite pastime of patrons is to sit outside and watch the trains rumble by. This is one of my favorite stops on the trip.

The next stop is Holbrook, once called the "hell-raising Babylon on the Little Colorado." It became the county seat for Navajo County in 1985. The Geronimo Trading Post offers a variety of souvenirs and information on stops along the Mother Road. Holbrook is home to the "other" Wigwam Village Motel. This classic Route 66 motel offers today's motorists much of the same quirky character it did in the 1950s. Vintage cars are parked outside most teepees.

The neon signs and rock-and-roll culture slowly faded as we temporarily abandoned the highway to photograph the muted colors of the Petrified Forest National Monument, where trees have turned to stone. The twenty-eight-mile loop road out of Holbrook descends into another world, one that tells a story 225 million years in the making. A stop at the Rainbow Forest Museum provided a map of stops along the way.

At the northern section of the loop, we crossed I-40, where there are remnants of the Old Route 66, mostly impassable. Here we entered the Painted Desert, shrouded in warm desert hues, and stopped at the Painted Desert Inn, a national historic landmark. It is a pueblo revival–style structure with cultural history exhibits.

It would take months to stop at the multitude of roadside sights and experience all that the Arizona towns have to offer. Our journey to Chicago would probably have taken a year if we investigated even a portion of the Route 66 icons and natural landmarks along the way.

With Arizona in the rearview mirror, the red rocks and picturesque mesas of New Mexico beckoned and we headed for Gallup.

Native American Handicrafts Galore

We waved goodbye to Arizona, embarking on the four hundred miles of Route 66 across the state of New Mexico. There are some realignments of the Mother Road ahead, much of the time forcing travel on I-40, and we anticipated several "off 66" destinations.

A stop in Gallup allowed us to enjoy the largest Indian center in the Southwest and the ceremonial capital of Native America. There are many Native American peoples in the Gallup/Four Corners region. By far the most numerous are the Navajos, who are today widely regarded for their achievements in wool, with original Navajo rugs and blankets (both new and antique) sought by private collectors and museums. Route 66 travelers have historically looked forward to stopping along the highway to buy Indian handicrafts. Gallup has come a long way over the past several years. Blighted areas still exist, but many vintage motels and cafés have been refurbished, giving the main street a modern look. Here a historic Route 66 icon, the El Rancho Hotel, draws visitors from around the world. Built in 1937, it was used as a base by movie crews during filming, and the rooms are named after big-name Hollywood stars. New to the town is the elaborate Fire Rock Casino, where we stopped to leave a donation for the Native Americans.

From Gallup, we temporarily abandoned Route 66 and headed south on Highway 602 to El Morro National Monument to hike a short trail to Inscription rock, a magical place of historical consequence. The lifesaving water in a constant pool at the base of a *cuesta* historically attracted those who traveled this trade route. These travelers inscribed their names into the wall, a sort of a guestbook spanning centuries. In proximity, there are visible signatures and messages left by the Anasazis, Spanish conquistadores, migrants traveling by wagon train or on foot and railway surveyors.

Winding back to Route 66, we arrived in Grants, a railroad town considered a true Route 66 location. Near here, the Mother Road crosses the Continental Divide. We settled into a KOA Kampground, where pizza from the "Kamp Kitchen" was delivered right to our trailer.

Route 66 is alive and well from Grants to Albuquerque. The details regarding pre- and post-1937 realignments in this area are confusing, so we chose to ignore them and merely enjoy the road.

The largest city in New Mexico, Albuquerque, is worth an extended visit to experience all the Native American and Route 66 sights. Walking through the old town plaza, we found ourselves surrounded by music and dancing in the park, curio shops and the pleasant aroma of chili and Mexican food, all in the shadow of the famed San Felipe de Neri Church. We made a creepy stop at the Rattlesnake Museum.

Albuquerque is home to the Rattlesnake Museum, which boasts the largest collection of different species of rattlers in the world. In addition, there are turtles, scorpions, tarantulas and a huge, scary black widow.

On a trek down Old Route 66 through Albuquerque's downtown area, we photographed numerous neon-clad eateries, but our favorite find was the statue of *Madonna of the Trail*, a monument dedicated in 1928 to pioneer mothers. This statue is one of a dozen along the National Old Trails and is a twin to the one located in Upland, California.

An Out-of-This-World Detour

New Mexico's Route 66 spans 604 miles, a figure that is complicated with old and new realignments. Leaving Route 66 as we know it, we headed for Santa Fe. Were we abandoning Route 66? Not exactly. When the Highway of Dreams was dedicated in 1926, it ran through the capital of New Mexico,

Santa Fe, following the Old Pecos Trail. In 1937, after losing reelection, a grumpy governor blamed his loss on politicians in Santa Fe and, in his remaining days in office, successfully set out to have Route 66 realigned to Albuquerque, thereby bypassing Santa Fe altogether.

Today, few Route 66 signs are found in Santa Fe, and the ones that do exist declare it as "Pre-1937 Route 66." Still, hundreds of old motels, such as the renovated El Rey Inn, are reminiscent of those so popular along Route 66 and remain in Santa Fe largely unnoticed in the shadow of the town's rustic and artistic culture. One such motel is the King's Rest Court Inn, complete with carports next to the rooms.

With its plaza, ethnic restaurants, Native American handicrafts and art galleries, it is tempting to stay in Santa Fe and not leave its boundaries. Numerous day trips are difficult to resist, such as visiting

At one time, enclosed garages and carports adjacent to motel rooms were all the rage. The King's Rest Court Inn on Old Route 66 in Santa Fe offers an opportunity for guests to get that retro experience.

the nearby Bandelier National Monument, the Bradbury Science Museum in Los Alamos, Abuquiu's Ghost Ranch (where Georgia O'Keeffe was inspired to paint her best works) and, to the north of Santa Fe, the famed Taos Pueblo, a photographer's dream.

Back to Route 66 as we know it today, we traveled through Cline's Corners, more than just a truck stop. The story goes that the gas station and trading post were moved when Route 66 was realigned in order to remain on the Mother Road. Today, as before, it is a favorite stop for travelers.

Once again, we abandoned America's Highway for a four-day stay in Roswell to attend the annual UFO convention. The town was filled with visitors from near and far sporting alien costumes, T-shirts and even dogs dressed as ETs participating in the alien dog contest. I was relegated to the back seat while the purple blow-up alien doll rode in front. We attended lectures, met abductees, watched Adrienne Barbeau of *The Swamp Thing* fame and waved with enthusiasm as the event culminated in a parade of out-of-this-world creatures marching down the main street.

Like a shining star in the winter sky, the Route 66 Auto Museum in Santa Rosa beckons visitors with a hoisted hot rod. More than thirty cars are featured, from vintage to classic to street rods.

Returning to Route 66, we passed through Sumner Fort to see two grave sites, each claiming to be the "real" plot where Billy the Kid's remains are interred. Reuniting with Route 66 at Santa Rosa, we toured the Route 66 Auto Museum, which features more than thirty cars from vintage to classic to street rods. There is even a motorcycle made of wicker. The town, located on the Pecos River, was the site of filming a portion of the *Grapes of Wrath* movie—there Tom Joad watched a train rumble across a bridge.

Our next stop, Tucumcari, brought us within striking distance of Texas. The Mother Road is lined with abandoned gas stations, cafés and motels. Probably the most famous is the Blue Swallow Motel. Decorated with murals, it is a favorite overnight stop for Route 66 travelers. The owner boasted that they are nearly filled to capacity much of the time.

We reached the Texas border with mixed feelings. It was difficult to leave the beautiful and historically exciting state of New Mexico, but as we entered Texas, we looked forward to many new adventures.

THE MIDPOINT CAFÉ: HALFWAY THERE

Texas has been good to Route 66. The Mother Road crosses the shortest section of the Panhandle, 178 miles in all. Of that, about 150 miles of Route 66 are still intact, although some sections are not paved. The Old Route generally follows I-40 as a frontage road and offers opportunity to drive in a leisurely fashion, without giant trucks running you down. Green fields and farmland hug the road, and the big blue Texas sky is dotted with puffy white clouds. The tale of the rise and fall of the Mother Road is written in dozens of small towns along the way.

Today, hundreds of abandoned and decaying buildings have surrendered to weeds and vandals. Garages, cafés, motels and gas stations are only shadows of what they once were. However, some have managed to continue, beckoning travelers to pull off I-40 for a meal or to fill up. One such eatery is the iconic Midpoint Café in the town of Adrian. Here a sign confirms that those motoring the length of America's Highway have reached the halfway point. We stopped for a meal to celebrate this milestone and enjoyed outstanding food and service.

Travelers following Route 66 know that they are at the halfway point when they reach the Midpoint Café in the town of Adrian, Texas. Of course, Mother Road memorabilia is sold in the café, and the staff enjoys talking about the history of the road.

In the town of Amarillo, we made the obligatory stop at Cadillac Ranch. Here, ten Caddies are stuck into the ground, tails up, covered with spray-painted graffiti while photographers snap away. We watched a mom and dad show their young child how to spray-paint graffiti and then tossed the empty can on the ground. I left disgusted.

The Texas town of Amarillo is known for its steaks, many of which we saw grazing roadside. The Big Texan Steak Ranch in this "beef capital of the world" offers a seventy-two-ounce steak for free, with one caveat: you must eat it, *and the trimmings*, before an hour passes. As a highlight of our Amarillo stay, the steakhouse sent a limo, which mooed like a cow and sported the horns of a bull, to the trailer park to pick us up. At the steakhouse, one poor soul was attempting to get a free steak and apparently missed the mark by three shrimp.

East of Amarillo, we stopped to photograph several spray-painted VW bugs, planted in a row at "the Bug Ranch," and continued on to Groom, which touts two claims to fame: the largest cross in the Western Hemisphere, which stands 190 feet tall, and a cockeyed water tower.

Eat a seventy-two-ounce steak, plus the trimmings, within one hour's time and it's free! Welcome to the Big Texan Steak Ranch in Amarillo, Texas. A limousine picks up campers at the nearby RV park and ferries them home after dinner.

Along Route 66, bigger is always better. The giant cross, touted to be the largest in the western hemisphere, rises 190 feet into the Texas sky. Nearby is another roadside attraction, a cockeyed water tower.

For many miles, we traveled on Route 66. On one side of us, vehicles on I-40 raced along, while the other side was lined with expansive fields of tall grass, wildflowers and massive grain silos.

Two rest areas near the town of Alanreed are sponsored by the Texas Department of Transportation and are well worth a rest. The one for westbound traffic features exhibits on the history of the area through the population growth after the invention of windmills and barbed wire fences. The eastbound rest area salutes Route 66 with several innovative exhibits, including an outside trail with a Route 66 History Walk and Time Line. Entering McLean, the last town in Texas bypassed by I-40, we stopped to photograph a Phillips 66 Service Station built in the 1920s, the first one in Texas, which operated for more than fifty years. The price on the pump was nineteen cents per gallon.

McLean is known for its Devils Rope and Old Route 66 Museum—everything you wanted to know about barbed wire. The theme is that barbed wire gave us control of the land, and windmills made the land habitable.

With Route 66 in the great state of Texas coming to an end, we stopped at Shamrock, a town that flourished when Route 66 was completed there in the 1930s, and visited the Tower Service Station and U Drop Inn Restaurant. At night, its neon is dazzling.

Just shy of the border, we perused the Pioneer West Museum located in the old 1925 Reynolds Hotel, which housed many a weary traveler for fifty years. Next door is the restored Magnolia gas station, with the old glass pumps intact.

As we left Texas, we enjoyed the slower pace of Route 66, part of which is paved with the original concrete. There was a time when gates were closed across some areas of the highway where it traversed through rangeland. Drivers were forced to open the gates and close them after passing through. With this in mind, we said goodbye to Texas.

Oklahoma: A Return to the 1930s

Bidding farewell to the Lone Star State of Texas, we were delighted to find that traversing many sections of Oklahoma's Route 66 threw us back to the 1930s. Miles of the Mother Road are paved with the original, pristine curbed Portland concrete, with interrupting asphalt patches. The *click clack* sound of the tires on the road reflects the sound heard by travelers of the past. These sections are like an outdoor museum, featuring the history of road construction, evolving pavement design and engineering.

In the early 1920s, all Oklahoma men between the ages of twenty-one and forty-five were required to perform four eight-hour days of road work each year. If they did not do their duty or find a substitute, a five-dollar road tax was assessed. When the state undertook the funding of local highways, this law was repealed.

It seems that almost every town in Oklahoma has at least one museum. Erick boasts the 100th Meridian Museum and the Roger Miller Museum, and a short hop to the east is Sayre's Railroad Museum. Top on our favorites list is the National Route 66 Museum Complex, composed of several museums, including Route 66 History, the Transportation Museum, the Old Town History Museum, the Farm & Ranch Museum and a windmill collection. Most all museums offer discounts for seniors and students, and the entrance fees are quite modest.

Further east is the Oklahoma Route 66 Museum in Clinton, which depicts the evolution of Route 66 and modern roads in that

Some portions of the Mother Road are paved with the original 1930s Portland concrete. Installed in sections, the road interacts with car tires, singing a click-clack song.

state, from animal paths to Indian trails, pathways of American and European explorers, army roads, cattle paths and railroad tracks. The museum actively collects stories from oldsters who traversed the road as youngsters. "We came down this road in September 1923. Mud roads and flash floods. Took us two months to get to California in a model T Ford," recalled ninety-six-year-old Nellie Kirseleith.

Reaching Oklahoma City, we tried to digest all we had learned from the multitude of museums visited during the day, taking shelter from a pending storm that had flooded several cities not far from where we were camped. Summer travelers should expect rainstorms and plan accordingly. Waking to a clear sky, we spent three hours at the National Cowboy and Western Heritage Museum located on top of Persimmon Hill. Numerous galleries exhibit breathtaking artwork depicting the American West, plus galleries featuring the American cowboy, western performers, the frontier West and American rodeo.

Northeast of Oklahoma City, Route 66 ribbons through green fields. In Arcadia, a sixty-four-foot-tall LED pop bottle beckons visitors to stop at

The Round Barn is one of the many roadside attractions along the route in Oklahoma. It was built by a farmer in 1898 and has since been restored. Visitors are invited inside, where Route 66 trinkets are sold.

"Pops" to purchase from a selection of five hundred varieties of soda, "a true Route 66 Icon." It is emblazoned in neon at night. Nearby is the famed Round Barn, erected by a farmer in 1898 and since restored. A bit farther east is the Oklahoma County 66 Auto Trim and Mini Museum. We snapped a photo of the sign and the blue whale replica.

Outrageous and creative roadside attractions are plentiful in Oklahoma, carrying over the tradition of Route 66's heyday.

Museums, a Whale and Andy's Hometown

It was high noon on April 22, 1898, when Oklahoma was choked with dust raised by fifty thousand people trampling the earth to claim "unassigned Oklahoma land" as their own. There were some cheaters in this land rush who showed up before the starting time to stake out their land. These people were called the "Sooners," and thus Oklahoma is known as the "Sooner State."

Oklahoma has preserved much of its stretch of Route 66. On the historic route, concrete-paved in areas, we continued to Wellston, traversing over a 1933 iron bridge, a trip back into time, while I-44 (a continuation of I-40) flew by at breakneck speed. Reaching Chandler, we visited the Museum of Pioneer History and a stop at McJerry's Route 66 Gallery. Unfortunately, Jerry McClanahan was not there to autograph the book he authored, the bible of our trip, *The EZ 66 Guide for Travelers.* We left him a cigar and continued on.

A stop at the Route 66 Interpretive Museum, housed in a former National Guard Armory built in 1936, welcomed us with beds, where visitors may recline and watch videos about the Mother Road. Near Stroud, we spied a surprising road kill: an armadillo! We photographed the old 1939 Rock Café. In Supulpa, it was a thrill to snap photos of a decaying drive-in movie theater and then traverse a 1929 iron bridge over Rock Creek. So deserted is this section of Old Route 66 that often it is possible to stop and take pictures without pulling off the road.

East of Tulsa, we visited the blue whale of Catoosa, which is touted in guidebooks as a must stop, and for good reason. Built in the early 1970s as an anniversary present, it is the result of more than 125 sacks of concrete. The leviathan rests in a moss-clouded pond that has historically

The giant whale of Catoosa is a widely publicized roadside attraction in Oklahoma that just may tug at your heartstrings. There is something strangely beguiling about this large cement whale.

served as a swimming hole for locals and Route 66 travelers. The whale appears rather beguiling as it invites visitors to step inside Geppetto-style.

I had been looking forward to visiting the town of Foyil, the hometown of Andy Payne, winner of the Bunion Derby. The 1928 footrace organized as a publicity stunt to promote Route 66 was launched from Los Angeles to New York, on Route 66 through Chicago. The winner was a Foyil High School graduate, part Cherokee. A plaque commemorates his success, and a bronze statue stands in a grassy field.

Just outside Foyil is the "world's largest totem pole," created by Ed Galloway in 1948. Expecting a cheesy grab for attention, we were surprised to find this endearing statue and its surroundings full of exquisite charm. The cement artwork is adorned with Native American depictions, including Geronimo and Sitting Bull. It sits on the back of a giant turtle and is surrounded by smaller poles. A victim of the elements, it is in the process of renovation.

Next we visited the little Oklahoma town of Miami to photograph the Route 66 Coleman Theatre Beautiful. Since 1929, it was continuously

The carved totem pole is a sight that attracts hundreds of travelers. The owners of the land where it sits are kind enough to welcome the crowds in the spirit of the Mother Road.

open for the entertainment of the townspeople. The owner donated the theater to the town, and it is now undergoing restoration.

Bidding farewell to the Sooner State, we slipped over a rather nondescript border and found ourselves at the start of Route 66 in Kansas, a stretch of only thirteen miles.

A Bit of Kansas, a Lot of Missouri

Kansas claims only thirteen miles of Route 66, but they are charming miles. The little town of Baxter Springs offers a loop across the unique and historic Rainbow Bridge, the last of three "Marsh Arch" bridges.

In the small town of Galena, a fun stop is 4 Women on the Route, a restored Kan-O-Tex gas station. This is where director John Lasseter and Pixar's Joe Ranft were inspired by the old rusty tow truck displayed there to create the Mater the Tow Truck character in the movie *Cars*. While there, we met a couple visiting from France driving the length of Route 66 westbound.

It takes only thirteen miles of Route 66 to cut through a corner of Kansas. However, there are charming sights to see. The historic Rainbow Bridge is the last of three "Marsh Arch" bridges on the route.

After a short jaunt through Kansas, it magically became Missouri. With no fanfare, we bid farewell to Oklahoma and Kansas and headed into the Show Me State to see what it would show us along America's Highway.

More than three hundred miles of Route 66 ribbon through Missouri in a diagonal direction. Lush green fields embrace the road, which continues through the heart of Joplin, touting such roadside amusements as a giant coke bottle and a humungous crayon. There are museums and parks galore. It is possible to stay on the Mother Road without resorting to Interstate-44 all the way from Carthage to Springfield.

Around Springfield, winding narrow roads wind through farms and ranches, the green fields alive with Queen Anne's Lace. There are two major attractions in Springfield in addition to the four-story Bass Pro Shop, which touts itself as a wildlife museum. First is Fantastic Caverns, not only a geologic wonder but also a bastion of colorful history. The cave tours are conducted via tram within the limestone walls.

Second is the Wilson's Creek National Battlefield. The Civil War Battle of Wilson's Creek in 1861, after a bitter five-hour struggle between Union and Confederate forces, left 2,539 of the 17,000 troops killed or

The 4 Women on the Route gas station is a restored Kan-O-Tex. Here there is an old tow truck sitting out front that reportedly gave director John Lasseter and Pixar's Joe Ranft the idea for Mater the Tow Truck in the movie *Cars*.

wounded. There is a museum and self-guided auto tour, with a ranger-guided visit to the 1852 Ray house, a field hospital for the wounded soldiers. It is a rather somber experience to look out over the peaceful countryside and envision the horrors it once held.

At my insistence, we drove some fifty miles from Springfield to a museum dedicated to author Laura Ingalls Wilder, and there we toured her home, which was left just as it was when she died in 1957. She lived there with her husband, Almanzo, and their daughter, Rose. Laura was in her sixties when she began writing about her childhood in a series best known as *The Little House on the Prairie*. Her books and the resulting television series are among America's favorite stories, and certainly mine.

Headed east on 66 through the manicured and fenceless yards of Marshfield neighborhoods, we enjoyed endless pastoral scenes and stopped to photograph the picturesque barns, churches, retro

In Mansfield, Missouri, some fifty miles off the route, tours are conducted through the home of Laura Ingalls Wilder, where the author lived with her husband, Almanzo. Here she wrote her famed stories of *The Little House on the Prairie.*

Known as the Mural Capital of the World, the Mother Road town of Cuba is a collection of artwork decorating the town's buildings. Each painting tells a historical story.

gas stations and historic bridges, such as the 1923 Route 66 bridge over the Gasconade River. Of course, there were plenty of roadside attractions, such as Waynesville's giant bowling pin and a half-size replica of Stonehenge at the University of Missouri at Rolla.

We missed the Giant Dripping Faucet in St. James but were tickled to see they have a vacuum museum. The Mother Road town of Cuba offers great neon signs and is primarily known as the "Mural Capital of Route 66." Unfortunately, the highly recommended Route 66 Café was not only closed but gutted as well.

Show Me Caverns, a Bridge and an Arch

Continuing through the Show Me State of Missouri, we arrived in Stanton, site of Meramec Caverns, which historically has been advertised along the route by signage on old barns. Those signs are now treasured

The Chain of Rocks Bridge in the Show Me State of Missouri exudes an unexplainable magical aura for those who walk the mile to emerge on the opposite shore in Illinois. One of the longest of the steel-truss bridges in the nation, it was built in 1929 and is the site of a scene in the movie *Escape from New York*.

Route 66 icons right up there with the Burma-Shave signs. The limestone caverns are decorated with breathtaking geologic wonders in addition to a colorful history that alleges that Jesse James used the area as a hideout. The campground at the caverns site is lush with grass and trees and sits on the bank of the Meramec River.

Between the caverns and St. Louis, Route 66 becomes confusing with pre- and post-1932 alignments that stop and go, passing under and over Interstate 44. In Allenton, there is a Six Flags theme park. Further east is Eureka, featuring Route 66 State Park located on the former site of the town of Times Beach, which was bought, dismantled and decontaminated after the discovery of widespread dioxin contamination. It is reportedly a safe place to visit today.

Leaving the small towns and beauty along 66, we drove into St. Louis, and the realities of civilization hit us by way of traffic, fast-food restaurants and malls. But along the great Mississippi River, we found a quiet oasis: the Chain of Rocks Bridge. This one-mile Route 66 river crossing was built in 1929, and a five-cent toll was charged. It is one of the longest steel-truss bridges in the nation and has a twenty-two degree bend in the middle. Today, it is reserved for walkers and bicyclists. Walk to the other side and you will emerge in Illinois. In the end, this bridge proved to be one of my favorite sites on the trip.

Getting high to view St. Louis seems to be a favorite pastime. The 630-foot Gateway Arch, the tallest monument in the United States, graces the left bank of the Mississippi. Construction was completed in 1965, and it has become a popular destination for visitors from all over the world. Small pods elevate visitors to the top, allowing views of the mighty Mississippi.

At the base of the arch is the Museum of Westward Expansion, which displays some of the rarest artifacts preserved from the 1805 expedition of Lewis and Clark. Set aside at least an hour to view the timeline exhibit, the world of the pioneers and the Native Americans. Just west of the arch is the 1839 St. Louis Courthouse, where the first two of the Dred Scott trials were held in 1847 and 1850.

Near St. Louis (but actually across the river in Illinois) is the Lewis and Clark Confluence Tower. The tour lifts visitors via elevator 150 feet to view the confluence of the Missouri and Mississippi Rivers. The 360-degree view helps understand the lay of the land.

Missouri is alive with the beauty of the Ozarks, the pastoral farmlands, the mighty rivers, the quaint townships and the sprawling cities. This state was originally acquired from France in the Louisiana Purchase. Although it is widely considered a southern state, it is actually in the Midwest.

As we cross the border into Illinois, the event is punctuated only by a sign. Here we realize that our trek from one end of Route 66 to the other is near the end. With that in mind, we drive into Illinois toward Chicago.

Illinois: Land of Lincoln and Ra66its

Headed for the eastern terminus of historic Route 66, we slowed down to digest the beauty and history of three hundred miles of the Mother Road in Illinois, the land of Lincoln. Hugging America's Highway through most of the state are cornfields, ranches and farms, as well as a strong dose of Mother Road spirit.

In the town of Staunton, we visited Henry's Ra66it Ranch, greeted by owner Rich Henry and Big Red, a plump, rosy, nose-twitching

Rich Henry loved visiting roadside attractions, so much so that he established his own. Today, he greets visitors at his Ra66it Ranch in Staunton, Illinois.

bunny. After touring Route 66, Henry decided that he wanted a quirky roadside attraction of his own. His ranch attracts visitors from all over the world. In the yard are half-buried Volkswagen Rabbits, an antique gas station with vintage pumps and signs from days gone by. Nearby is a quaint St. Paul Lutheran Church, home of the Neon Cross of Route 66. Rich gave us the grand tour and embraced us with his friendly, easygoing demeanor. It was one of our favorite stops.

After photographing Shell gas pumps dating back to 1926 at a restored Soulsby Station in the town of Mount Olive, we walked around a somber historical site. The Union Miners Cemetery is dominated by an impressive monument dedicated to Mother Jones (1830–1930), who "gave her life to the world of labor." She is buried with the victims of the October 1898 Battle of Virden, part of the larger mine wars that established Illinois as the leading union state in the country.

Route 66 is celebrated with gusto in the little town of Litchfield. The Ariston Café is one of the oldest along the Mother Road. Founded in the nearby community of Carlinville in 1924, it was relocated to Litchfield.

A monument dedicated to Mother Jones (1830–1930) anchors the Union Miners Cemetery. Jones is said to have given her life to the world of labor.

The Ariston was inducted into the Route 66 Hall of Fame in 1992, as was the nearby Sky View Drive-In, which remains open today.

Springfield is dedicated to the memory of Abraham Lincoln. His childhood home and tomb are located there. The Lincoln Museum and Library warrants a several-hour visit. Springfield is also the birthplace of the hot dog on a stick, which is served at the Cozy Dog. It was purportedly invented by Ed Waldmire Jr., father of the recently deceased Bob Waldmire, the famed Route 66 artist. Ed began selling the dog in 1946 at the Illinois State Fair, where it gained popularity. Also in Springfield is Bill Shea's Historic Gas Station and Museum. For a few bucks you can chat with Bill and marvel at his collection of Route 66 and gas station memorabilia.

One of our very favorite Route 66 communities is the little town of Atlanta, which lies under the protective watch of a giant yellow happy

Many Route 66 icons adorn the small town of Atlanta, Illinois. Watching over the town is a statue called, variously, *The Bunyon Man*, *The Hot Dog Man* and even *The Muffler Man*. He was moved to Atlanta from the nearby town of Cicero, also on Route 66.

face painted on a water tower. A Route 66–trekking Christian motorcycle group was eating breakfast at the 1934 Palms Grill Café, which has been refurbished but retains gems from the past, such as its vintage cash register.

Across the street stands a muffler man statue holding a giant hot dog. He is affectionately called the Bunyon Man. An impressive thirty-foot-tall clock tower stands in front of the 1908 town library. The clock, a 1909 vintage Seth Thomas, is the community's labor of love. Local volunteers hand-wind the clock three times a week.

With these unique little towns in our rearview mirror, we head for the big city, the windy city, the city where Route 66 ends—or begins, depending on which way you travel.

A JOURNEY ENDING AT THE BEGINNING

After a month of travel, and more than 2,400 miles along America's Highway, we arrived in Chicago, greeted by its impressive skyscrapers, traffic and noise. Admittedly, after just a few hours in the windy city, we

One of Chicago's famed Route 66 icons is Miller's Pub, where Frank Sinatra once sang "My Kind of Town (Chicago Is)."

fell in love with the architecture, waterways, public art, variety of shops and friendly people.

Route 66 seems to have been forgotten by Chicago, a fact that has challenged David G. Clark, an official guide and Mother Road enthusiast. Clark is dedicated to keeping Chicago's stretch of the road alive through research, articles in the National Historic Route 66 Federation newsletter and his recent publication, *Exploring Route 66 in Chicagoland: Journeys Through History on the Mother Road in Cook County, Illinois.* On a walking tour, he pointed out surviving Route 66 icons such as Miller's Pub, where Frank Sinatra sang "My Kind of Town (Chicago Is)." We did manage to find one "End of Historical Route 66" road sign.

Before embarking on the trip home, we reflected on the month-long journey we had finally completed, the sites we had visited, the people we met and the challenges we overcame.

The Route 66 part of our journey was at a conclusion, but the fond memories shall endure. Returning home, we eventually hooked up with

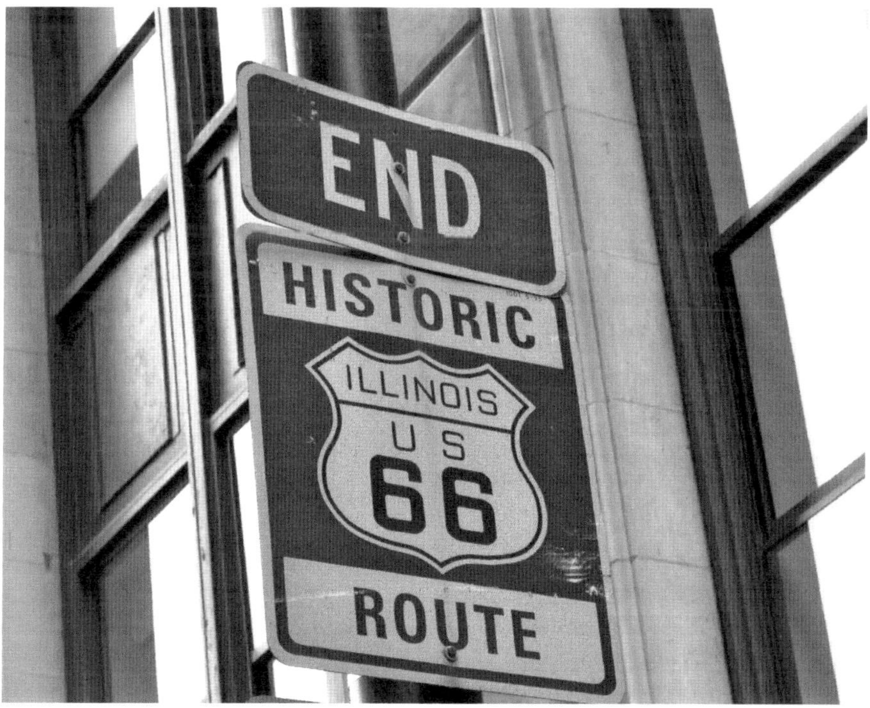

This sign marks the end of Route 66. Or does it mark the beginning?

another historic route: that of Lewis and Clark, which we loosely followed to its terminus at the Columbia River on the border of Washington and Oregon States.

MISSION ACCOMPLISHED

If you dream of traveling back in time along Route 66, you may find that the tickle can grow into an itch that begs to be scratched. Despite high gas prices and time commitments, the trip is definitely doable. Having traveled in the past few years to Mexico, Italy, Egypt and Africa, we found our journey within the United States to be comparatively safe and easy. Our national infrastructure, though we may complain, is generally excellent. The people, whatever their political or life views, are friendly and enjoyable. Our museums are inexpensive and first class. And nowhere on the trip did we find a lack of facilities, gas, water, directions, signs, restrooms or satisfactory lodging, whether motel or RV park.

The trip home took us through Iowa to South Dakota, Mount Rushmore, Crazy Horse, the Badlands, Custer State Park, Devils Tower, Deadwood and Sturgis. However, the beauty of the nation did not end there. Our travels through Wyoming, Idaho, Montana and Washington State were awesome, as was the trip down the Oregon coast.

Back in California, we could not bear to bring our adventure to an end. We followed the Klamath River Road to Happy Camp, where my sisters and brother live, and then went on to Lava Beds National Park, down Highway 395 to our favorite fishing spots in the Eastern Sierra's Owens Valley.

At last, the trip of a lifetime ended, and we backed our trailer into the driveway. Once home, we waded through bags of souvenirs, thousands of photos and a ton of fond memories. We had seen America's heartland from that historic road that for decades has been paved with hope, adventure and soul. We had decided on an ambitious project and seen it to completion. We had lived peacefully together in a small trailer without the amenities of home. We now know firsthand why Route 66 is coveted in the hearts of those who traveled it, in the past and the present. The road continues to beckon.

About the Authors

The oldest of seven children, Claudia grew up in Hollywood, California, and graduated from Los Angeles City College with an AA degree in journalism. Living in Duarte, California, for the past thirty years, she has become engrained in the community, serving as president of the Duarte Historical Society and Museum for the past twelve years. She is a former president of the Duarte Woman's Club. For more than ten years, she has authored a biweekly column for the *Star News*, a section of the *Pasadena Star News*. Her columns feature people, events and history of the Duarte area.

Growing up in Silverlake, California, Alan earned a BA degree in biology at California State University, Los Angeles. He currently serves as president of Duarte's Public Access Channel (DCTV) and is a former commissioner of the Duarte Parks and Recreation Commission. Alan is a member of the Westerners Corral of History Writers and E Clampus Vitus, a historical society that places history plaques throughout the West. He is also a former president of the Underwater Photographic Society. His photographs have appeared in many professional publications, including *Westways* magazine and *Skin Diver* magazine. Alan is retired from his career in sales.

Married for forty-seven years, Claudia and Alan have raised three children and are currently enjoying five grandchildren. As a family, they loved camping throughout the United States. Since retirement, Alan and Claudia purchased an eighteen-foot trailer and have spent much of their time exploring the western United States, especially the Southwest, the Eastern Sierras and the National Mojave Preserve areas. In 2010, celebrating their sixty-sixth birthdays, they headed east on Route 66 to Chicago, writing a series of newspaper articles about the Mother Road for the San Gabriel Valley Newspaper Group.